The Uncertain Trumpet

The Uncertain Trumpet:
a History of Church of England
School Education to AD 2001

Norman Dennis

Civitas: Institute for the Study of Civil Society
London

First published August 2001

© The Institute for the Study of Civil Society 2001
The Mezzanine, Elizabeth House
39 York Road, London SE1 7NQ
email: books@civitas.org.uk

ISBN 1-903 386-13-6

Typeset by Civitas
in New Century Schoolbook

Printed in Great Britain by
The Cromwell Press
Trowbridge, Wiltshire

For if the trumpet give an uncertain sound who shall prepare himself to the battle?

I Corinthians xiv, 8.

To our dear grandchildren

Robert and Sarah in England
and Max in the United States

Contents

Author

Norman Dennis was born in 1929 in Sunderland, one of the four sons of a tram-car driver. He was educated at Green Terrace Elementary School and the Bede Collegiate Boys' School. He won a place at Corpus Christi, Oxford, but chose to go to the London School of Economics, where he was awarded a First Class Honours in Economics. He was Reader in Social Studies at the University of Newcastle upon Tyne. He has been a Rockefeller Fellow, Ford Fellow, Fellow of the Center for Advanced Study in the Behavioral Sciences at Palo Alto, Leverhulme Fellow, and Visiting Fellow at the University of Newcastle upon Tyne. He is currently Director of Community Studies at the Institute for the Study of Civil Society.

With Professor A.H. Halsey he is author of *English Ethical Socialism,* Clarendon Press, 1988. Civitas is the current publisher of his *Families Without Fatherhood* (with George Erdos), 3rd edn., Civitas, 2000; and *The Invention of Permanent Poverty*, Civitas, 1997. He edited and with Detective Superintendent Ray Mallon contributed two chapters to *Zero Tolerance: Policing a Free Society,* Civitas, 1997, and contributed 'Beautiful Theories, Brutal Facts: the welfare state and sexual liberation' to *Welfare, Work and Poverty* (edited by David Smith), Civitas, 2000. He is also well known for his study of a Yorkshire coal-mining town, *Coal Is Our Life* (with Cliff Slaughter and Fernando Henriques), Eyre and Spottiswood, 1956, and two participant-observation studies of bureaucracy and politics as they affected the working-class district of his birth, Millfield, Sunderland, *People and Planning*, Faber and Faber, 1970, and *Public Participation and Planners' Blight*, Faber and Faber, 1972.

He has been a Sunderland city councillor and is active in his ward Labour party. In collaboration with Ann and Peter Stoker and George Erdos he is currently studying the struggle between the bureaucratic, political, academic and media advocates of drug permissiveness and their opponents.

Foreword

Are we in the middle of a culture war? Few doubt that since the 1960s many Western countries have lived through a major social and cultural transformation affecting attitudes to crime, children, the family and marriage, as well as social class, race and religion. How best can we understand these changes?

Writing in the 1830s Tocqueville predicted that one of the dangers for free societies was that they would become too individualistic and provide fertile ground for a new kind of despotism under which the state would take upon itself alone the task of meeting the wants of its people, who would seek constantly to 'procure the petty and paltry pleasures with which they glut their lives'. Its power would be like that of a parent, said Tocqueville, if its object were to prepare people for adulthood. But, in reality, its aim was to prepare them for perpetual childhood. Such a government was happy for people to rejoice, 'provided they think of nothing but rejoicing'.[1] It deepened and extended the control of government and diminished the capacity of individuals for self-rule.

Today, many writers believe that Western societies have been in the midst of such a transformation, at least since the 1960s. Some have called it a culture war.[2] In Tocqueville's time, Western societies were protected from hyper-individualism by strong churches and a vibrant civil society which allowed people to pursue public purposes in common with like-minded others, and to remain true to common values whilst respecting individuality. Subsequently, the influence of these 'mediating structures' has been weakened.

Does this analysis hold true for Britain? *The Uncertain Trumpet* by Norman Dennis is the first in a series of publications which will explore the issues central to the culture war. Although the book focuses on church schools, it is an analysis of the society-wide transformations which radically altered the social and cultural landscape of Britain during the twentieth century.

David G. Green

x

1

State Subsidy and State Control

The Purely Voluntary Efforts of the Church of England

At the beginning of the nineteenth century in England there were charity schools and Sunday schools. But there was no school education for the children of masses of poor people. In 1811 three old-fashioned High Churchmen, Joshua Watson, Henry Norris and John Bowles, managed to found a society to remedy this state of affairs, the National Society for Promoting the Education of the Poor in the Principles of the Church of England.[1] This was the beginning of a movement by which, through their voluntary contributions of money and effort—for the first 22 years with no state assistance at all—members of the Church of England built schools in every old Church of England parish in the land.

The National Society obtained the goodwill of the Archbishop of Canterbury, Charles Manners-Sutton. He took the chair at the Society's inaugural meeting on 16 October 1811, and he presided over its fortnightly meetings whenever he could. Voluntary donations poured in from well wishers within a short time of its foundation. HM Inspector C.K. Francis Brown reported that with few exceptions the clergy took a deep interest in the schools. Some vicars taught in school both in the morning and the evening. Some taught when the teacher was away. Some made up the teacher's salary from their own pocket.[2]

A survey by the National Society in the 1840s showed that the parish clergy were not only largely responsible for founding schools, but also, as Francis Brown had reported, sometimes for financially maintaining them. 'The expense falls mainly on the vicar.' 'The incumbent has built three

cottages, which he has converted into schoolrooms and a
dwelling for the mistress at his own expense.' Often these
schools, run on a shoestring, were in small and dark
buildings, 'more picturesque without than convenient
within', as an Archbishop of York wrote in 1947. The
teachers were frequently untrained,[3] 'and their methods
would cause a present-day educationist to cry out with
dismay'. But the majority of poor children who received any
school education at all had it given in these schools.[4]

The First State Grants and the Beginning of State Control

The Parliamentary Committee on the Education of the Lower Orders 1816-18

In June 1816 a parliamentary committee reported that 'a
very large number of poor Children are entirely without the
means of Instruction, although their parents appear to be
generally very desirous of obtaining that advantage for
them'. 'Your Committee has observed with much satisfaction, the highly beneficial effects produced on all those parts
of the Population which, assisted in whole or in part by
various Charitable Institutions, have enjoyed the benefits
of Education'. The committee said that 'the greatest advantages would result in this Country from Parliament taking
proper measures, in concurrence with the prevailing
disposition in the Community, for supplying the deficiency
of the means of Instruction which exist at present, and for
extending this blessing to the Poor of all descriptions'.[5]

In its second report the same committee observed that 'in
all the returns, and in all the other information laid before
them, there is the most unquestionable evidence that the
anxiety of the poor for education continues not only un-
abated, but daily increasing'.

The committee was firm on the primacy of the principle
that schools should be provided, if possible, by private
organisations. 'Wherever the efforts of individuals can
support the requisite number of schools it would be unnecessary and injurious to interpose *any* parliamentary assistance.'

Even in many poor neighbourhoods, the committee said, private subscription could be raised to meet the yearly expenses of the school. But private subscription in such places could not meet the cost of the initial purchase and erection of the schoolhouse. The committee suggested, therefore, 'that a sum of money might well be employed in supplying this ... want, leaving the charity of individuals to furnish the annual provision'.

But there were also numerous districts where no aid from private exertions could be expected. The committee therefore recommended the adoption of the Scottish parish-school system. The state should provide the school. The ratepayers should then meet the annual salary of the teacher of £20 a year, a sum 'so very trifling', that it was never made the subject of complaint by any of the ratepayers in Scotland.[6]

The state made its first annual schools grant of £20,000 to the National Society and the British and Foreign Schools Society in 1833. It was a contribution to the cost of school buildings, not teachers' salaries or other school purposes. The bulk of the money went to the National Society, for it had most of the schools.

The Committee of the Privy Council on Education 1839

In 1839 a Committee of the Privy Council for Education was set up. The prime minister, in setting up the council, raised the issue of purely state-financed schools. There *was* a role for state schools, he said, to cater for 'a large class of children who may be fitted to be good members of society without offence to any party—I mean pauper orphans, children deserted by their parents, and the offspring of criminals and their associates'. It is from this class that 'the thieves and housebreakers of society' were continually recruited, and that had filled the workhouses with the ignorant and the idle.

He warned, however, that being educated in some schools was worse than having no school education at all. 'It sometimes happens', he observed, 'that the training which the child of poor but virtuous parents receives at home, is but ill-exchanged for the imperfect and faulty instruction which he receives at school, debased by vicious association.'[7]

The Committee of Council immediately appointed inspectors. Their instructions were to 'ascertain the number and character of schools for the children of the poorer classes'.

As a protest against state inspection, Joshua Watson, the leading spirit in founding the National Society, resigned from his post of treasurer after nearly 30 years. G.A. Denison, another principled opponent of the state control of the Church of England's voluntary schools—now only partly voluntary schools because they were state supported—wrote to the Clerical Inspector of Schools:

> My dear Bellairs,
> I love you very much; but if you ever come here again to inspect, I will lock the door and tell the boys to put you in the pond.[8]

From 1843 state grants became available for furniture and apparatus as well as for school building, and for the building of denominational teacher-training colleges.

The state grants were for *working-class* education only. Working-class education in the nineteenth century had a clear identity. The concept of a ladder out of the working-class system was not hinted at until the late 1860s, was not defined until the 1870s, and was not substantially acted upon until the twentieth century. The code governing state grants for schools still, in 1860, defined their purpose as that of promoting 'the education of children belonging to the class who support themselves by manual labour'.[9]

According to Lawson and Silver, in spite of the commitment of the Committee of Council to religious education generally, the Committee of Council's autonomy and authority were 'bitterly resented by the Church of England'. Church of England suspicions of creeping state control were justified in 1846, when the Committee of Council began to lay down conditions for the management of Church of England schools.

The Church of England was still able to 'force' important concessions from the Committee of Council when it felt that the state was usurping Church of England functions.[10] For example, the Church of England opposed a proposal that the Committee—the state—should establish and supervise a college for training teachers. The proposal was dropped. The Church of England also secured an arrangement under which the inspectors of Church of England schools should be appointed only with the approval of the Archbishops of Canterbury and York.[11]

But the concessions to the Church of England were perceived as bias against themselves by the Nonconformists. Many of them had regarded the creation of the Committee of Council favourably, 'as a step leading away from the power which the Church of England wished to usurp, of educating the whole people', John Bright said in 1847. 'But from 1839 to this year we have found no step taken by the Government which has not had a tendency to aggrandise the Established Church.'[12]

It was therefore the Nonconformists, under the influence of Edward Baines, the editor of the *Leeds Mercury*, who initiated the so-called 'voluntaryist' movement. The 'voluntaryists' were totally opposed to any form of state intervention on anybody's behalf. The Congregational Board of Education and the Voluntary School Society broke away from the British and Foreign School Society, and *refused* government grants. By 1853 the Congregational Board had 431 schools. Baines, 'the backbone of the movement', wrote a temporarily influential book in which he used statistics to prove the success of 'voluntary Christian zeal' in providing the means of educational and religious instruction, even for a rapidly rising population.[13]

The Newcastle Commission 1859-61 rejected universal compulsory state education as both unattainable and undesirable, even though not more than a quarter of the children in inspected schools in 1858 were receiving a 'good' education. (The standards in uninspected schools—the majority—were likely to be much lower.) In the opinion of the Newcastle Commission, the practical results of voluntary efforts in this country, mainly by the denominations—and therefore mainly by the Church of England schools—compared well with the compulsory system as seen, for example, in Prussia. The results in Prussia and in other states with systems of compulsory state education did not

appear to be 'so much superior to those which have already
been achieved among ourselves by voluntary efforts'.[14]

On the commissioners' recommendations, each child was
to earn a state grant for the school of 4s a year (20p) on the
basis of attendance and 8s subject to examination. Money
was forfeited if the child failed to satisfy the inspectors in
reading, writing and arithmetic. The loss was 2s 8d a year
(13p) for each subject failure. The 'revised code' of the
Newcastle Commission—payment by results—became an
object of widespread vilification, and more than a century
later still powerfully resonated in left-wing circles, along
with Peterloo, the Tolpuddle Martyrs and the Means Test.
But this concentration on literacy and numeracy, and
payment by results as assessed by state inspectors, could be
praised by secularists, as it was by John Hurt, as at least a
victory of the state over the churches.[15]

A 'voluntaryist' minority on the Newcastle Commission,
led by Edward Miall, was still expressing the belief that the
annual state grants should be gradually withdrawn.[16] But
the inability of the voluntary system to raise the financial
and human resources to achieve more or better schooling
beyond a certain point led to the collapse of the purely
'voluntaryist' movement. Baines confessed to a change of
heart in 1867, and Miall gave his support to the National
Education League, founded in 1869, whose programme
included secular education, rate support and compulsory
school attendance.[17]

Purely State Schools

The Case for State Schools before 1870

The importance of state education—at least state-subsidised
elementary schools for the poor —had been preached at the
end of the eighteenth century by diverse thinkers, including
some of the strongest exponents in general of *laissez-faire*,
such as Blackstone, Adam Smith, Eden, Malthus, and
Bentham. State school systems had been set up in Prussia
by Frederick the Great, following the example of his father;
by the Empress Maria Theresa in Austria; by Turgot in

France; and by Florida Blanca in Spain. England was almost alone in late-eighteenth-century Western Europe in leaving the education of the poor to the charity schools and Sunday schools.

The early Church of England schools, under the auspices of the National Society, had been set up in the ancient parishes of the kingdom. But the new manufacturing towns and mining districts presented a new problem.

According to Sir Spencer Walpole, in 1818 only about one in four children of the poor were at that time receiving school education of any kind.[18]

The Factory Commission Report of 1834 contains a table giving returns from factories. Of the workers in Lancashire mills, 83 per cent could read (a notable achievement in literacy). But 62 per cent of Lancashire workers could not write. In Yorkshire 85 per cent could read, but 52 per cent could not write. In Cheshire the percentage able to read was even higher, 90 per cent, but 53 per cent could not write.[19]

It was taken for granted that a state school would provide religious and moral training, as well as instruction in reading and writing, and this vital element, too, was missing. In 1842 the Children's Employment Commission found that:

> neither in the new colliery and mining towns ... nor in the towns that have suddenly sprung up under the successful pursuit of some new branch of trade or manufacture, is there any provision for education by the establishment of schools with properly qualified teachers, nor for affording the means of moral and religious instruction and training, nor for supplying the spiritual want of the people; nor is there any provision whatever for the extension of educational and religious institutions corresponding with the extension of the population.

'Unconscious, invisible, hidden' discrimination and 'exclusion' are burning topics in the year 2001. There was nothing unconscious or hidden about the exclusion of some working-class children from school educational opportunities in the nineteenth century. In 1842, in mining districts of Derbyshire, where there *were* a few free and National schools, colliers' children were *formally excluded by the rules*.[20] In 1842 a factory inspector, Leonard Horner, reported that in an area of 32 square miles of the densely populated new industrial districts of Oldham and Ashton, with a population of 105,000, there was not a single public day school for the education of poor children.[21]

The Hammonds give an account of the self and mutual education of the otherwise unschooled 'English workman' during the industrial revolution.

The English workman, the Hammonds write, sought in co-operation with his workmates the education necessary for 'a larger life'. The role of permanent victim faced with the insuperable obstacles of material deprivation and social discrimination did not exist in his cultural repertoire. He created his own educational organisations, and developed them under the fierce discouragement of his rulers.[22] He was educated, too, by the powerful pamphleteers of the time, who without exception preached self-improvement and mutual improvement as the solution to the problems of the working class. Almost without exception these pamphleteers rejected self-pity as a personal response and mob violence as a weapon. The most notable of them was William Cobbett (the paragon of the self-educated poor man), a genius whose papers and pamphlets were 'read with all the greater zest' because they were 'forbidden by a power that could punish disobedience with swift and arbitrary strokes'.[23]

State Schools from 1870

Forster's Act of 1870 established the principle of direct state school provision. Lord Standon's Act of 1876 prohibited the employment during school hours of any child under the age of ten living within two miles of a school, including a Church of England 'National' school. This introduced, *de facto*, compulsory school attendance. The Act of 1891 abolished school fees in all schools charging less than 10*s* (50p) a year. The Elementary Education School Attendance Act 1893 raised to 11 the age at which any child could gain partial or total exemption from compulsory school attendance. The state was now committed to providing or underpinning a system of free, universal and compulsory school education.

The Dual System

The 1870 Act introduced purely state schools. But it was within a system of co-operation between the state schools and the Church of England schools (and other voluntary schools receiving state grants).[24] The 1902 Education Act transferred state education from the School Boards of 1870 to the counties and county boroughs established in 1888. The 1902 Act reaffirmed that English education was a 'dual system' of state schools and voluntary schools aided by the state.

In the first of the Hadow reports, that of 1926, the Board of Education's Consultative Committee recommended that the state should facilitate further co-operation with the Church of England in the provision of schools.[25] One of the consequences was that the Education Act of 1936 made provision for grants (of from 50 per cent to 75 per cent) to assist the Church of England to reorganise the rest of the system into primary and senior departments ('special agreement schools' under the Act), with the age of transfer at 11.

For a time the Church of England schools continued to flourish side by side with the new schools. But the advantages given by local taxes to the Board schools (and the council schools they became after 1902) in meeting the demands of the state were very great. The Church of England could not afford to erect the spacious buildings required by the educational ideals of the late nineteenth and the twentieth century.

Between 1902 and 1938 the Church of England lost 2,620 schools. Every year about 100 were closed or surrendered to the state. The numbers of children taught in Church of England schools diminished both absolutely and in relation to the increase in population. In 1938 there were 10,100 council schools and 9,100 Church of England schools in England and Wales. The pupils in council schools numbered 3.5 million, in Church of England schools 1.25 million.

In 1939, William Temple, as Archbishop of York, chaired a committee on the relationship between the state and Church of England schools. This was followed by a survey of Church of England schools. In September 1942 the National Society produced a memorandum based on Temple's report. This was accepted by the Church Assembly in February 1943. Temple insisted that there should be no further surrender of Church of England schools, and no dilution of their distinctive ethos.[26]

In 1941 Temple and the Archbishops of Canterbury and Wales published their 'five points' on religious instruction in schools. Religious instruction ought to be given in all schools, whether Church of England or state. In all such schools, the day was to begin with a collective act of worship. There should be an 'agreed syllabus' of religious instruction. Parents would continue to have the right to withdraw their child from the school's religious events and from the religious instruction provided by the school.

In 1943 the first Diocesan Education Committees Measure (revised in 1955) laid the foundation for the Church of England's post-war work. In that same year the white paper was issued that foreshadowed the 1944 Education Act.[27]

The Lure of the Wholly State-funded School

A committee was appointed in the Diocese of Worcester just before the second world war broke out. Although it recommended that the Church of England schools for younger children (today's 'primary' schools) ought to be retained, its arguments suggested that in the secondary sector they were not so essential.

The committee argued that it was 'a well accepted principle of religious education that the early years of a child's life are of primary importance'. The link with the Church of England, and the fact that the clergy were in close personal contact with the teachers and the youngest children, 'provided an atmosphere, and prompted loyalties, which seem to us of great value'.[28]

But (by clear implication) these links, these loyalties and this atmosphere were not so crucial in the schools for the older children; they could cope with the state school. A factor that weighed heavily in this tendency to abandon secondary education to the state was the high quality of Christian education given in the state schools. 'Excellent religious instruction', the committee said, was given in most council schools. Under elementary education re-organisation schemes large numbers of the older children, in accordance with that belief, were moved from the Church of England schools to the senior council schools.

The very success of the Church of England in influencing the government in respect of the religious clauses of the 1944 Act acted as an incentive to give up Church of England schools altogether. The main pressures were finding the resources of money and commitment.

By 1947 the case for abandoning the Church schools altogether was being aired by senior figures in the Church of England. Again, the assumption was that England had little to fear, within England, from bad behaviour. The Archbishop of York, Cyril Garbett, said that, 'unavoidably', most of Church of England schools would be taken over by the local education authorities. The cost of alteration and maintenance of buildings was growing. The demands of the state, the paymaster, were increasing. Parents contrasted 'the humble accommodation of the Church school with the palatial buildings erected by the local education authority', and were usually indifferent as to the special type of religious education given to their children. Many of the laity now regarded Church of England schools as an unnecessary financial burden. The clergy doubted their value under changed conditions.

The historical argument that had influenced the Worcester diocese was generalised to all schools. The satisfactory state of religion in the local authority schools, 'brought about by the work of over a century since 1811', made surrender seem more acceptable.

The following is a statement from an inter-war pamphlet:

We enter into the benefits of generations of advancing Christian civilisation, and are thus saved from many pitfalls which were the daily temptations of our fathers. The failures today are not those of gross breaches of conduct like reeling drunkenness, riotous living, theft, and other glaring sins. The sentiments of modern social life are sufficient to kept us from those offences.[29]

In Garbett's opinion in 1947, agreed religious syllabuses in the wholly state schools were likely to prove an adequate foundation for a Christian nation. In that case, 'Churchmen may feel that their own schools have done their work for the nation'.[30]

No one would dream of expressing such sentiments today. The Home Office's annual volumes *Criminal Statistics England and Wales* show that the *increase* in the annual crime rate 1990-1991 was almost as much as the *total* annual crime rate even as late as 1960.

There was probably a higher volume of one type of private violence, namely, violence in the interests of the maintenance of the community's values, in the interwar period as compared with the year 2001. Some of this private violence, far from being criminalised, was permitted or condoned by the state.

Within limits set down by school rules and public opinion, teachers caned pupils. Subject to the neighbourhood's views of what was reasonable in all the circumstances, parents smacked their own children. With 'fair play' enforced by the onlookers, fisticuffs would settle matters between 'the best fighter' in the school or class and an incipient school bully. 'Respectable' men fought in the back lane in front of a crowd in order to stop other men swearing in front of women in the public house or the working men's club. (More frequently it was sufficient only to threaten to fight.) Good order at football matches was maintained by the strong likelihood that 'bad behaviour' would be dealt with by similar means by nearby spectators coming unhesitatingly to one another's assistance. In a place like Sunderland, where nearly every working man wore a flat cloth cap, on reasonable suspicion of an unaccompanied boy's misbehaviour any man could strike him on the upper arm with the cap's rubber peak. (The gesture that the cap was about to be taken off the man's head was nearly always sufficient to put an end to the incident.)

There is a multitude of contentious questions of psychology and social organisation that lie behind the justification and condemnation of such violence, as well as an absence of reliable facts on its prevalence and effects in the past.

But what has undoubtedly increased in prevalence is the violence that individuals or gangs inflict on other people in the pursuit of their own interests, whatever those private interests might be—money, glory, excitement or revenge. When figures more reliable than those provided by *Criminal Statistics England and Wales* became available through the institution of the British Crime Survey in the early 1980s, they showed that between 1981 and 1999 there was a 40 per cent increase in informants telling the interviewer that they had been the victim of some form of criminal violence. Robberies increased from 164,000 in 1981, to 183,000 in 1991, and to 353,000 in 1999. In the whole of the period 1920-38 the worse year for robberies in England and Wales was 1932, when the figure was 342. In the best year, 1927, there had been only 110.[31]

It is difficult in 2001 to realise how 'civilised' and 'Christian' England felt between the two world wars. In 2001 the crime figures of the interwar period are either ignored or rejected as false. But contemporary social comment and the social settings of films and novels support the amazingly low crime figures, not the modern academics and journalists who dismiss them as 'a golden age that never existed'.

The Trade-off between Subsidy and Autonomy

The 1944 Act modified the 'dual system' in ways that could be regarded as advantageous to the Church of England. Under the new arrangements the state provided more in subsidies for Church of England schools. The Act also allowed a trade-off of the level of state subsidy against the level of state control. The Church of England schools, as maintained voluntary schools, could opt to belong to the controlled school, or to the aided school category. There was more funding for, but more state control of, the voluntary *controlled* schools. There was less state support, but greater independence, for the voluntary *aided* schools.

For both controlled and aided schools, the local authority was responsible for all running costs, including staff salaries, interior repairs, maintenance of playgrounds, playing fields, and buildings used exclusively for school health services and school meals.

In the controlled schools, one-third of the governors (the 'foundation' governors) were appointed by the voluntary body. The teachers were appointed by the local authority. They could only be dismissed by the local authority.

Religious instruction was to be taught in the state schools in accordance with the non-denominational agreed syllabus, but denominational religious education could be taught in the voluntary controlled schools if requested by parents. If denominational teaching was provided, then the governors had a voice in the appointment of a 'reserved' religious-instruction teacher.[32] Only two Roman Catholic schools opted for this 'controlled' category.

In voluntary aided schools both worship and religious instruction could be entirely denominational. Aided schools normally made use of the syllabus recommended by the diocese, but governors were free to decide to use the syllabus of another diocese, or the agreed syllabus of the state schools. Some Anglican schools had regular though infrequent celebrations of the Eucharist to which parents were invited.[33] Two-thirds of the governors were appointed by the voluntary body. In return for this degree of autonomy, the managers or governors were responsible for capital expenditure on such physical alterations as the local authority might require. They were also responsible for expenditure on external repairs to school teaching buildings.

The controlled and aided schools did not have to find all the money for the capital expenditure for which they were responsible. From 1944 to 1959 they had to find 50 per cent of their share of the expenditure.[34] From 1959 to 1967 they had to find 25 per cent. From 1967 to 1974 they had to find 20 per cent.

In the early 1970s the National Society and the Board of Education of the General Synod jointly examined the increasingly serious position of financing Church schools.[35] In 1974 the state subsidy was raised once more, so that only 15 per cent had to be found by the school.

For many of the early years of the operation of the 1944 Act, the Church of England had a powerful ally at the heart of the Ministry of Education, J.L.B. Todhunter, of the Legal Branch. According to the National Society, he did not simply assist, he 'displayed zeal for' Church schools and their financing.[36]

The late 1980s saw the beginning of the trend to strengthen the Church of England's depleted rights to run its 'own' schools—now, as we have seen, very heavily subsidised by the state—as it saw fit. In the schools in the controlled category, in appointing the head teacher the governors were required to 'have regard to' the candidate's ability and fitness as head teacher to preserve and develop 'the religious character' of the school. In schools in the more autonomous and less subsidised aided category, the governing body was legally permitted to discriminate in favour of committed members of the Church of England in making any of its teaching appointments.

It was also made easier financially to move out of controlled status into aided status, with the greater freedom that gave to the school to create its own distinctive Church of England character. The creation of School Organisation Committees and Admission Forums increased the ability of the Church of England to affect admissions policies, and to influence any proposals to establish, close, or change the category of a school.[37]

Under the Education (Schools) Act 1992 the inspection of denominational worship and education (that is, religious education other than according to the locally-agreed syllabus) was made the responsibility of school's governing body, not HM Inspector of Schools.[38]

In the case of controlled schools, the foundation governors only chose the denominational inspector. The denominational inspection covered collective worship and, if requested by the governing body, social, moral, spiritual and cultural education. In the case of aided schools the whole governing body chose the denominational inspector. In aided schools the denominational inspection covered religious education; collective worship; and social, moral, spiritual and cultural education.[39]

State-supported Pluralism?

In February 2001 the Dutch ministry of justice published the results of the International Crime Victims Survey (ICVS), which it had co-ordinated. The findings were based on interviews with 35,000 people in 17 countries. The survey identified low-crime countries such as Japan, Finland and Switzerland. Canada, Denmark and the United States were among those identified as medium-crime countries. England and Wales, Australia and Holland were classified among the high-crime countries. A few days before, a study of 60,000 teenagers in 30 countries had shown that English teenagers were at the top, or near the top, of all lists of drunkenness and the consumption of illegal drugs. The study, the European School Survey Project on Alcohol and Other Drugs (ESPAD), showed that one in three English boys aged 15 to 16 had been drunk at least 20 times.[40]

The *Guardian* interviewed 16-year-old girls who were among the brightest in their GCSE class. They lived in Suffolk, but had travelled to Manchester for the night out. 'On a school week, if they only go out three times, they drink about 12 litres of alcopops and smoke 150 cigarettes each. 'We are no different to your average teenagers ...', said Zoe. 'Everyone's on pills. But I don't touch heroin because I saw my teenage sister's best friend die from a heroin overdose ... We come from a nice village ... There's nothing to do except drink....'

Neville, 16, goes to sixth-form college in Manchester, where there is an excess of activities for teenagers, 'but the best thing is getting lagered'. 'Once a week', [he continues], 'we aim to get totally bladdered... I drink ten cans of lager and half a bottle of brandy in shots. Then I do an eighth of weed. The others, who are 16, drop pills, like ecstasy.'[41]

By the end of the twentieth century, 68 per cent of all pregnancies in Liverpool were outside of marriage. In Southwark the figure was 66 per cent, in Sunderland 62 per cent. Among girls under the age of 16, half of the pregnancies ended with an abortion. Few of the pregnancies ended in marriage; in 1997, when there were 8,300 underage pregnancies, none.[42] In May 2001 Marie Stopes International (MSI) published the results of a survey of 907 17-19 year olds in the United Kingdom who had been on at least one overnight supervised school trip at the age of 16 or younger. Twenty per cent said they had had 'full penetrative sex' on such a trip. Sixty-six per cent of those who had had full penetrative sex said they had used a condom. Dr Marianne Parry, MSI's Medical Adviser, said that it was thus 'great' to see so many young people 'being responsible'. 'The safer sex message is obviously getting through', she said. But a quarter of those who had had full penetrative sex had not used contraception. Dr Parry said that this was what was 'really worrying' about the findings.[43]

Unmarried English girls under the age of 18 had the highest rate of pregnancies in western Europe. It was twice the rate of German girls under the age of 18, and three times the rate of French girls. The state, of course with the most difficult cases, had the worst record of all of care for girls. One quarter were pregnant when they left 'care', and a further quarter were pregnant within two years of leaving 'care'.[44]

In a characteristic response, the *Guardian* said that there was 'widespread concern that efforts to tackle the problem of teenage parenthood should not be reduced to *moralising*'.[45] The *Guardian* did not say whether there was also widespread concern that the lack of 'moralising' rather than an excess of it was an important contributor to the problems of crime, disorder, drunkenness, drug consumption, underachievement at school, underage pregnancy and pupil parenthood.

But it was the education system itself that experienced the consequences at first hand of the success over the previous 40 years of those who had been 'concerned' that morality along with religion-as-faith should be expelled from the schools. It seems to be for that reason, that it and the nation's children were in the front line, that parts of the education system slowly, slightly and reluctantly started to turn back to consider the importance of a school's 'ethos', the current synonym for what had become the new 'love that dare not speak its name', morality.

In February 2001, a Department for Education and Employment green paper proposed that schools *should* develop their own ethos. The green paper proposed that the contribution that the government made to Church of England and other 'faith' school building programmes should rise further, from 85 to 90 per cent.[46]

Beyond society's deserts, therefore, the opportunity was offered for faith schools to redeem the errors of the past, or to bring to fruition the efforts that they had persevered in against the spirit of the times. Whether in 2001 that opportunity would be seized or sucked dry by the forces that had brought England to its present pass was ... in the lap of the gods.

2

Christianity in State Schools

Before 1870: the Identity of Religion and Education, and the Unity of the State and the Church

The Dark Ages and the Middle Ages

From the first days of the Celtic monks and St Augustine's mission to these islands[1] until well into the nineteenth century, all education in church, school or university, that is, all formal education, was religious education. Education for getting a living and preparation for other secular pursuits took place in the home, the neighbourhood and in association with workmates and masters. Who can stand now in Eton college chapel and not be astonished through its sheer physical magnificence and beauty at the weight given to religion at the end of the middle ages?

The decretals of Pope Gregory IX in 1234 ordered each parish priest to have a clerk, one of whose duties was to keep a school to which his parishioners were to be admonished to send their sons.[2]

Bishops issued constitutions setting out what the priest's clerk should teach: the ten commandments, the creed, the seven works of mercy, the seven deadly sins, and so on. The most authoritative syllabus of religious instruction of this kind was prescribed in the provincial constitutions of 1281. *Ignorantia sacerdotum* specified the articles that had to be expounded to the parishioners in the vernacular four times a year. *Ignorantia sacerdotum* of 1281 was reissued on several occasions, for the last time in 1518.[3]

The Reformation

Henry VIII's royal authority was exercised to ensure that cathedrals had schools, and that they were fully under the control of the deans and chapters. 'Edward VI grammar schools' give Edward VI an undeserved reputation, for the schools that bear his name were often founded at the cost of older and larger educational establishments. But Archbishop Cranmer largely determined the educational policy of his reign. Every cathedral church had to have its own grammar school. The Bible in English made its way into the schoolroom. For the unschooled in church, as well as the formally educated, the Prayer Book of 1549 contained a catechism, simply written, that represented the minimum of knowledge of all adherents of the Church of England—from time to time, that is, of all English people.[4]

After the accession of Elizabeth, education was much more rigorously manipulated to secure adoption of the new national church. Her royal injunctions of 1559 ordered that no man was to teach unless he had been granted a bishop's licence as to both character and orthodoxy. In 1571 this rule became part of the canon law of the Church of England. In 1604 candidates for a teacher's licence, whether teaching in school *or privately in a gentleman's household*, had to subscribe to the Royal Supremacy over the Church in England, the Book of Common Prayer, and the Thirty-Nine Articles. 'Education was still regarded as essentially a religious activity.'[5]

Until the Civil War in the middle of the seventeenth century, formal education was under the sole auspices of the Church of England. But whether strictly under the control of the Church of England or not, the prevailing belief was that without religion—in England, Christianity—at its heart, education could not take place at all.

The English Reformers not merely accepted the mediaeval conception of all formal education as religious education; they intensified it. The tumults of the 1640s and 1650s, however, reinforced in the ruling class the view that *too much* schooling among the population at large was a danger to the established order.[6]

The Eighteenth Century

At the end of the seventeenth and in the eighteenth century, such elementary schools as were available for the mass of the population were provided by Christian philanthropy and private enterprise. By 1700, the philanthropy that since the Reformation had founded grammar schools was now providing, by endowment and public subscription, rather, elementary schools. The years between 1699, when the Society for Promoting Christian Knowledge (SPCK) was founded, and 1730, by which time its efforts in this field were weakening, saw the expansion of philanthropic education for the very poorest children.

The SPCK encouraged public subscription as a mode of the charitable financing of schools. Its primary objectives in doing so were moral and missionary. It aimed to combat vice and profanity, and to propagate *Anglicanism* at home and abroad. Here is an example of a pro-forma for making a subscription to a charity school:

> Whereas *Prophaneness* and *Debauchery* are greatly owing to a gross Ignorance of the Christian Religion, especially among the poorer sort: And nothing is more likely to promote the Practice of *Christianity* and *Virtue*, than an early and pious education of Youth: And whereas many *Poor People* are desirous of having their Children Taught, but are unable to afford them a Christian and useful Education: We whose names are underwritten agree to pay Yearly, at Four equal Payments, (during Pleasure) the several and respective Sums of Money over against our Names respectively subscribed, for the setting up of a *Charity School* in the Parish of ... for Teaching [*Poor Boys*, or *Poor Girls*, or] *Poor Children* to Read, and Instructing them in the Knowledge and Practice of the Christian Religion, as profess'd and taught in the Church of *England;* and for Learning them such other Things as are suitable for their Condition and Capacity.[7]

In the 1780s, the Sunday-school movement was launched by Robert Raikes, the editor of the *Gloucester Journal*. (Two hundred years later the parades of Sunday school scholars still crowded the centres of provincial cities on Good Fridays—with an orange each for reward.) The purpose was to teach poor children to read the Bible, and 'to train up the lower classes in habits of industry and piety'.[8] The Wesleyans in particular opposed the teaching of writing in Sunday schools.[9]

The success of the Sunday schools helped to prepare the way for the weekday schools for the poor. The schools movement within the Church of England in the late eighteenth century grew from an awareness of the influence of the philosophers of the French Enlightenment, and of the industrial changes conventionally dated from 1760—which was indeed a date that ushered in a host of innovations. But its objective was neither to accept the new ideas nor adjust to the new conditions. It was to warn against the social and moral dangers they carried.

The objective of Church of England philanthropists was to reinforce traditional religious codes of behaviour. They intended to redeem an apathetic Church, to educate an illiterate populace, and to protect the threatened social order.[10] While Wesleyan Methodism made its educational appeal directly to the poor, the educational movement in the Church of England was anxious to win the support of the influential and the great. Wilberforce, one of the Church of England's most influential spokesmen in social matters, said that he wished to 'do within the Church, and near the throne, what Wesley had accomplished in the meeting, and among the multitude'.[11]

These active Christians in Methodism and the Church of England—the 'evangelicals'—formed themselves into organisations to press their social reforms. The Society for the Suppression of Vice, for example, prosecuted sellers of licentious and obscene books (which they took to include anti-religious political works, like those by Thomas Paine).

Hannah More, one of the original 'blue stockings', a friend of and on terms of equality with the intellectual luminaries of her time like Samuel Johnson and Edmund Burke, was the leader of the evangelical educators in the Church of England. As every pupil who has taken a GCSE in the history of the period knows, she too considered writing an unnecessary accomplishment for the poor. The evangelical educators believed in the subordination of those in a lower station in life, just as did the lax clerics they attacked. But unlike the lax clerics, they believed in taking active measures to achieve it.

The evangelical tracts were simple moral tales, illustrating basic Christian virtues and the rightness of the social order. Two million of Hannah More's tracts were reputed to have been sold in the single year 1795. Whether sold or distributed, there certainly seems to have been a considerable market for her ideas. The popularity of Hannah More's work led to the formation of the Religious Tract Society.

The Nineteenth Century

G.M. Trevelyan warned the mid-twentieth-century readers of his history of England—before the radio was in every home, and when television had entered scarcely any—to beware of the feelings of superiority they might harbour of being 'well educated' just because they had been to school and their ancestors had not. 'Though much was lacking in the organised education of that age as compared with our own', Trevelyan writes, 'very many people of all classes at the time of Waterloo knew the Bible with a real familiarity which raised their imaginations above the level of that insipid vulgarity of mind which the modern multiplicity of printed matter tends rather to increase than diminish.'[12] Ordinary people were educated by their ballads and tales:

> Ranging and ringing thro' the minds of men,
> And echoed by old folk beside their fires
> For comfort after their wage-work was done.[13]

Nevertheless, there was continuing concern about the impiety, ignorance and immorality of the working class (though not only of the working class), and to combat them the 'National Society for Promoting the Education of the Poor in the Principles of the Church of England' was founded in 1811.[14] For 146 years thereafter it was to be the main educational instrument of the Church of England. After it was replaced by the Synod's Board of Education, the National Society remained an important force in Church of England school education. In the words of an appeal for contributions in 1823, it sought to 'confer upon the Children of the Poor the Inestimable Benefit of Religious Instruction, combined with such of Acquirements as may be suitable to their Station in Life, and calculated to make them useful and respectable Members of Society'.[15]

But other views were being formulated and acted upon. The great independent ('public') schools under the inspiration of Thomas Arnold's régime at Rugby gave Christianity a central role. But some middle-class secondary education was being reformed to better suit the demands of science, commerce and industry: a University of London without religious tests for entry was founded in 1830. *Secular* education had made its appearance on the scene.

The Parliamentary Committee on the Education of the Lower Orders 1816-18

The success of the Church of England National schools since 1811 had raised the problem of 'two opposite principles' in school provision. These were the subject of consideration by the Parliamentary Committee on the Education of the Lower Orders, appointed in 1816. One principle was that of 'founding schools for children of all sorts'. The other, the committee said, was providing schools 'for those only who belong to the Established Church'.

So long as there were sufficient resources to build two schools, one upon each principle, 'education is not checked by the exclusive plan being adopted by one of them'. But in places where there was only one school, and the education provided in it effectively excluded Dissenters or Roman Catholics, they were deprived of *all* means of school education. (The question of adherents of other faiths or of atheists did not arise.)

The committee reported, however, (with the 'greatest satisfaction'), that in many Church of England schools only the children of Church of England parents were required to learn the catechism or attend church. All that was required from 'sectaries' were assurances that the children should 'learn the principles and attend the ordinances of religion, according to the doctrines and forms to which their families are attached'. The committee found that the Roman Catholic poor were also anxious to avail themselves of Church of England schools, so long as they were not required to learn the catechism, or share in any religious observance. The committee expressed the hope that in these circumstances, of the Roman Catholic faith of the children not being compromised or diluted, the Roman Catholic clergy would 'offer no discouragement to their attendance' at Church of England schools.[16]

The Parliamentary Committee on the State of Education 1834

Parliamentary interest in education was stimulated by the Reform Act of 1832, and in 1833 the first state subsidy for school buildings was approved—£20,000 a year to be paid as grants in aid of private subscription. The money was channelled through the National Society and the British and Foreign Schools Society.

In 1834 the National Society's secretary, the Rev. J.C. Wigram, gave evidence to a parliamentary committee on education. The question was again raised—is the Church of England, in providing schools, entitled to use them to promote the principles of the Church of England among those who came to be instructed in them, or should it be providing them for all the population? Could the second be undertaken without making the school completely neutral and inactive with regard to the promotion of the principles of the Church of England?

Wigram maintained that any set of people who wanted to educate their children could and should organise themselves to do so. They could and should make the sacrifices necessary if they wanted to run schools in accordance with their own views of what constituted a sound education.

But the weakness of his position, now that his organisation was in receipt of state aid, was immediately exposed by his interlocutor. The Church of England school was now a quasi-state school. What kind of 'religion', if any, was a *state* school entitled to put before its disparate pupils?

What is the position *now*, Wigram was asked, when the Church of England receives a portion of the parliamentary grant of £20,000 a year for its million pupils? Can not the state now for that reason *require* the Church of England schools to be open to all, on terms acceptable to all or offensive to none?

Although you now have a million scholars ... do you not think it is desirable that some additional system should be introduced, which should be more comprehensive of the youthful population at large?

If there are a sufficient number of Dissenters in any place there may be a Dissenters' school and a Church of England school.

Supposing there is not a sufficient number of Dissenters ... might you not regulate your institution to include them?

I do not know how they could give up so much as would, in the eyes of Dissenters, make them more acceptable than they are now.

That is to say, the persons who have established these schools think it of greater importance to adhere to their peculiar plan, than to teach the whole population?

They find their plan working admirably well. They do not find the difficulties alluded to in your question, and say let well alone...

There is no doubt the right of each denomination to educate its own children from its own resources; *but if aid comes from the public purse, the question is, whether that aid should be offered to schools that comprehend all classes ...*

I do not like to give an opinion ... I am only concerned with one sort of school both officially and on principle.[17]

The Rev. William Johnson, clerical superintendent of the National Society, took it for granted that pupils choosing to come to Church of England schools should receive a Church of England education, and thought that other people took that for granted too.

What are the general rules ... with respect to religious instruction in the schools of the National Society?

They are taught according to the doctrine and discipline of the Church of England.

None are allowed to come to the schools without?

The question has never started; the impression is such that those who come there are instructed in the liturgy and catechism of the Church of England.

Henry Brougham, by now the Lord Chancellor, Lord Brougham and Vaux, was asked about free and compulsory state schooling as compared with voluntary societies, providing at their own expense an education they considered appropriate to voluntary pupils.

Do you consider that the aid or interference of the Legislature is required ... ?

Much good may be done by judicious assistance; but legislative interference is to be ... very cautiously employed because it may produce mischievous effects.

Do you consider that compulsory education would be justified?

I should regard anything of the kind as utterly destructive of the end it has in view. ... education would be made absolutely hateful ... They who have argued in favour of such a scheme from the example of a military government like Prussia, have betrayed ... great ignorance of the nature of Englishmen.[18]

The National Society was much the largest of the voluntary education societies, and its schools attracted the largest share of the state grant, which was distributed according to the amount of voluntary contributions raised. The Nonconformists saw the grant, therefore, as disproportionate state support for Church of England propaganda among the young. Charlotte Brontë's *Shirley* gives an account of rival school feasts, when the column of Church of England schoolchildren, 'priest-led and women officered', its band playing *Rule Britannia!*, marches at quick step down the narrow lane. They scatter the column of Dissenting schoolchildren and their pastors, who raise a feeble hymn and turn tail.[19]

The Committee of the Privy Council on Education 1839

To supervise the proper use of the (by present standards) minuscule parliamentary grant, but in order to keep education out of parliamentary controversy, the Committee of the Privy Council for Education was established—the Department for Education in embryo.

In his letter setting up the Committee of Council, the prime minister, Lord John Russell, emphasised the importance of Christianity in schools. He said that all inquiries had shown a deficiency in religious instruction, general instruction, moral training, and education in the habits of industry 'among the poorer classes'. This deficiency was not in accordance with the character of 'a civilised and Christian nation'. It was Her Majesty's wish that the youth of the kingdom should be religiously brought up, he said.

The rights of conscience had to be respected. But *in practice*, Lord John Russell said, the problems of exclusion and refusal to make concessions in the schools to other denominations and to those who believed in secular schools were not as serious as controversialists made them appear. The voluntary societies were not always exclusive, and the secularists were not always indifferent to religion.

One of the Committee of Council's important assumptions was that instruction in Protestant Christianity was '*the main element* of their work'. An 1846 Minute noted that 'the "classics" of the poor in a Protestant country must ever, indeed, be the Scriptures; they contain the most useful of all knowledge'.[20]

One of the Committee's inspectors argued in his report that if the 'legitimate' educator did not provide moral and religious instruction for children, then the vacuum would be filled by 'the publisher of exciting, obscene, and irreligious works' and by anyone who could 'readily declaim upon false and pernicious dogmas and principles'.[21]

A separate educational initiative was taken by the so-called 'ragged school' movement. The ragged-school movement, too, was driven by evangelical zeal. It, no less than the denominational societies, was concerned with educating its pupils in 'virtue' as well as knowledge. As Horace Mann said in his report on education following the 1851 Census, the ragged schools sought to convert 'incipient criminals to Christianity'.[22]

The Newcastle Commission 1861

The Newcastle Commission was appointed in 1858, and reported in 1861. The problem of single school areas was once again raised. Is any organisation *in receipt of state funds*, national or local, entitled to exclude anyone, by the principles it itself embraces, from wishing to participate in the service it provides? In places too small to allow the establishment of other schools, it is sometimes the case, the commissioners said, that the only one to which the children of the poor may resort, is 'under regulations which render imperative the teaching of the Church catechism' and attendance at a Church of England service. In such cases people of other denominations cannot attend without sacrificing conscientious convictions, They cannot avail themselves of educational advantages '*to which as taxpayers they contribute*'.

The majority of the commissioners came down heavily in favour of the school open to all comers. They described exclusion through the school requiring of all participants adherence to its own firm principles, without concessions to would-be participants, bluntly as 'an evil'. But they hoped that its removal would not require state regulation. It should result, if possible, from 'the curative influence of public opinion'.

But should public opinion not remove the evil, then 'it may be the duty of the Committee of Council to consider whether the public fund placed at their disposal ... may not be administered in such a manner as will insure to the children of the poor in all places the opportunity of partaking in the benefits *without exposing their parents to a violation of their religious convictions*'.[23]

1870: 'No Distinctive Catechism or Formula' in Wholly State-supported Schools

The position of the Nonconformists in relation to the teaching of Church of England Christianity, 'non-sectarian' Christianity and no Christianity at all is recorded in the *Inquirer* of 18 June 1870. A meeting was held in St. James's Hall, Manchester. Its purpose was to oppose denominational and sectarian teaching *when it was at the cost of the tax- and ratepayer*. The meeting approved the motion that, in schools established or aided out of the rates, there must be a prohibition on the use or teaching of any catechism, formulary, or tenet in support of any sect.

In seconding the motion, the Rev. C.H. Spurgeon said that he would never let his Nonconformity outride his Christianity, and if the Bible were excluded, he would 'preach defiance of the government up and down the land'. (There must have been some support for purely secular education in the hall, for some 'No, noes' were mixed with the cheers.)

Spurgeon also told the gathering that the question ought never to have arisen: it would have been better if the state had left education alone. 'It was a gross falsehood to say that voluntaryism had failed.'[24]

The situation for Church of England Christianity in schools was, therefore, transformed in 1870. In addition to having to grapple with the perennial problem, since 1833, of the claims of non-Anglicans to admission and freedom from Church of England education now that its schools were in part 'state' schools in receipt of state aid, from 1870 it had to consider, as the state church, what religious education should be in schools paid for *entirely* by the state.

Before 1870, the Church of England had had as its rivals the Nonconformists with their 'British' schools. But so far as school education was concerned, the Nonconformists took Christian school education nearly as much for granted as did the Anglicans.

Now a new educational force, the *wholly* state school, had entered the field, and in resources and number of pupils it was soon to dominate it. The new School Boards had the power to build schools and to control the education within them. There was, increasingly, a new element in public opinion to contend with, principled secularism. The National Education League, based in radical Birmingham, was a powerful lobby for secular school education.[25]

The Education Act 1870

In his speech introducing his Education Bill, W.E. Forster pointed out that only two-fifths of working-class children between the ages of six and ten years were on the registers of the voluntary grant-aided schools, and only one third of those between the ages of ten and 12. 'Our object is to complete the present voluntary system, to fill up gaps, ... welcoming as much as we rightly can the co-operation and aid of those benevolent men who desire to assist their neighbours.'

He then dealt with the conscience clause, allowing pupils in any school, wholly-state or part-state aided, to be withdrawn by their parents from any instruction and worship contrary to the parents' religious convictions. After a limited period, he announced, the existence of a conscience clause in the regulations of voluntary schools would be a condition for the receipt by any elementary school of public money.[26]

The 1870 Act laid no legal duty on the new state schools, the Board schools, to provide either religious worship or religious instruction. In practice, however, it was almost unknown for Board schools not to provide both.

As an outcome of fierce struggles, then, in which the proponents of purely secular education played some, but not a large part, under the Education Act of 1870 there was in fact Christian teaching in the new Board schools. But any religious teaching or worship that did take place had to be under the terms of the so-called Cowper-Temple clause. This provided that 'no catechism or religious formula which is distinctive of any particular denomination shall be taught in the school'.

As we have seen, the conscience clause itself was the solution suggested as long ago as 1818, as a way of accommodating non-adherents with strong faith, without having to dilute the faith of the accommodating school. But the 1870 Act had both a weakening of the 'faith' that the state school was allowed to offer and a conscience clause for every school in receipt of a state subsidy.

This met the wishes of the Nonconformists. It did not meet the wishes of many Anglicans and Roman Catholics who by their rates were compelled to support schools in which it was illegal for their children to be taught Christianity, the true faith, as they understood it to be. Non-sectarian Christianity was offensive to them. In the eyes of many, it amounted to the religion of a new Christian sect, with the school teacher as priest.

In the aftermath of the 1870 Act, however, the concept of the purely secular state school gained credence even in Nonconformity. In reporting on a conference of Nonconformists in Manchester on secular state education as early as 1872, the *British Quarterly Review* said that there were few even among Dissenters who were prepared for the enthusiasm with which the resolution was adopted, that 'the conference *unanimously and unfalteringly* took its stand on "the secular platform"'.

The argument that won the approval of the conference was that, while it was natural for the Church of England to insist on the competence of the state to teach Church of England Christianity in the state-financed schools, according to Nonconformist principles the state was charged with the care only of man's temporal interests. It had no kind of equipment for other service. State law was unfit to further the ends of religion.

Until 1870, the conference was told, Nonconformists had had a clear choice. It had been open to them to invite the state to take part in the education of the people. If that had been the choice, they were bound to require that the state schools limit themselves to secular teaching. It had been open to them, alternatively, to take the voluntaryist stance, and demand that religious teaching be an integral part of school education. If that had been the choice, Christian school education would have had to be the work of the Christian voluntary agency, with no role for the state.

With the 1870 Act the die had been cast in favour of state-provided and state-subsidised schools. The state schools and state-subsidised schools existed, and would continue to exist, in large numbers. A few Nonconformists 'might sullenly maintain the old ground of voluntaryism', a speaker said, but they would exercise no influence on the post-1870 course of events.

The 'incompetence of the state' in religious matters was a widespread notion. A British army officer who took part in a large survey during the first world war of the religious beliefs of soldiers said that we, the various denominations and Churches, had 'shirked our task and given ease to our consciences by letting the state take on the burden of religious education'. 'The state', he added, 'is not qualified to do so.'[27]

Nevertheless, the difference that adherence to a particular religious tradition made to an individual's life and to society was regarded as so profound that Nonconformists also continued for long to run schools on their own religious principles with the aid of state funds. In addressing the students of Westminster and Southlands teacher training college in the 1880s, Charles Garrett said that it was the belief in *immortality* that made a Wesleyan lay an *infinitely* high value on the well-being of *every* child. The meaning of every human life was transformed by the fact that the human being can never die, and that the school was preparing the pupil for eternity.

The scientific view of the material world did not affect that 'overwhelmingly important fact', as Garrett called it. 'Professor Huxley says that our educational ladder should have its foot in the gutter, and its top in the university. We say that our ladder should have its foot in the home, and its top in Heaven.' Children should be cared for by Christian parents in infancy; should enter a Christian school; pass through it to the Church militant; and on to the Church triumphant. By 'Christian' the speaker meant, of course, Christian as understood by his own sect.[28]

In 2001 it is difficult for most people to take seriously what divided Christianity from other faiths and from atheism, and what divided the Christian denominations from one another. It is difficult, therefore, fully to comprehend how seriously the divisions were in fact taken. Of course Hinduism and Sir Richard Burton's disgraceful *Kama Sutra* were not to be thought of, any more than any other of 'ye beastly devices of ye heathen'.[29] But also, as compared with their own Anglican, Roman Catholic, Wesleyan, Primitive Methodist, Congregational, Presbyterian, or Baptist beliefs, the beliefs of other denominations, or belief in a vacuous general 'Christianity', were hardly Christianity at all.[30]

In the event, the Methodists, the main Nonconformist providers of state-subsidised sectarian schools, adopted a policy of reducing their number. At their peak in the nineteenth century there were 900 maintained Methodist schools. By the year 2000 there were 57, half of them being run in partnership with the Church of England.

The Cross Commission 1888

By the mid-1880s both the Roman Catholic Church, led by Cardinal Manning, and the Church of England, were dissatisfied with the way the 1870 Act was working. In response to Cardinal Manning's complaints, backed by the Church of England, a Royal Commission was set up under Richard Assheton, the first Viscount Cross.

The Cross Commission took evidence from secularists who wished all religious teaching and observance to be banned from elementary schools. What struck the commissioners was that 'even those witnesses who strenuously advocated the secularisation of public elementary education most emphatically declared that they regarded religion as the true basis of education', and contended for its exclusion only in the belief that 'it could be provided in some other and better way'.

The Cross Commission concluded that it was 'of the highest importance' that pupils in the state schools should receive Christian and moral teaching. The Commission regarded any separation of the teacher from the religious teaching of the school as injurious to the morals and secular training of the pupils. What was more, 'the moral character of the *teachers themselves* would suffer if they were forbidden from giving religious instruction'.

In Christian schools of a denominational character in receipt of state funds, to which parents of a different denomination had no choice but to send their children because the neighbourhood had only one school, the parents of a different denomination had to have the right to require an effective conscience clause. Care had to be taken to see that the children should not suffer *in any way*, the Cross Commission said, in consequence of taking advantage of the conscience clause.

The Cross Commission provides a vivid insight into the condition of religion (or hypocrisy, or both) among teachers in late-Victorian times. The commissioners write that the testimony they had received from the state schools led them to believe that 'as a body' teachers would consider it a 'great loss' if they were debarred from giving Bible lessons. They regarded them as being among 'the most interesting and profitable to their scholars'.[31]

The minority on the Cross Commission, however, were already foreshadowing the secular future, and demanding that all parents should have the *right*—and the *power*—to send their child, if not to a secular school, then to a school where no particular version of Christianity was taught.[32]

1902: *Civic Virtue without a Religious Underpinning*

By the end of the nineteenth century religious views of the world and supernatural forces were losing ground to secular philosophies. But these secular philosophies, in so far as they impinged on the state and state-supported schools, set standards of morality for the ordinary person no less high, and sometimes much higher, than the everyday Christianity of the time.

The Elementary Code of 1904

In introducing the 1902 Education Bill, A.J. Balfour said that the success of its provisions depended upon ending the 'barren controversies' between the Christian denominations. The matter was settled so far as the wholly state schools were concerned. We had, he said, 'repudiated responsibility' for teaching any particular form of Christian religion in them. The education system had to now ensure the removal of other bases of 'denominational squabbles' in education.

The New Code of 1904 incorporated the changes that followed from the 1902 Balfour Act. Its introduction set out the classic statement of the aims pursued by public elementary education—working-class education—in England in the first half of the twentieth century. 'The purpose of the state elementary school', the Code stated, was to 'form and strengthen the character and to develop the intelligence of the children entrusted to it.' Though their opportunities were brief, school teachers could do much 'to lay the foundations for conduct'. By example and influence, aided by the sense of discipline which should pervade the school, the school teachers should attempt:

> to implant in the children habits of industry, self-control, and a courageous perseverance in the face of difficulties; they can teach them to reverence what is noble, to be ready for self-sacrifice, and to strive their utmost after purity and truth; they can foster a strong respect for duty, and that consideration and respect for

others which must be the foundation of unselfishness and the true basis of all good manners; while the corporate life of the school, especially in the playground, should develop that instinct for fair play and for loyalty to one another which is the germ of the wider sense of honour in later life. In all these endeavours the school should enlist, as far as possible, the interest and cooperation of the parents and the home in a united effort to enable the children not merely to reach their full development as individuals, but also to become upright and useful members of the community in which they live, and worthy sons and daughters of the country to which they belong.[33]

The Education Act 1918

In introducing the Bill that became the 1918 Education Act, the tone of the President of the Board of Education, H.A.L. Fisher, is the same as that of the author of the 1904 Code. Many working-class people, he said, were now seeking 'the treasures of the mind'.

These treasures of the mind were 'an aid to good citizenship, a source of pure enjoyment and a refuge from the necessary hardships of life spent in our hideous cities of toil'. Education was the education of the whole man, and the whole man was a spiritual being first, an intellectual being second, and a sensual being last.

But this emphasis on 'spirituality' was on an essentially secular, not religious spirituality. As it was secular spirituality, the state had little compunction about using compulsion to achieve it. The Bill proposed eight hours a week compulsory education after elementary school age. Such compulsion on young workers, overriding what they would choose for themselves, was 'no sterilising restriction of wholesome liberty'. It was an 'essential condition of a larger and more enlightened freedom', which would tend to stimulate the civic spirit, to promote general culture and technical knowledge, and to diffuse a steadier judgement and a better-informed opinion through the whole body of the community.[34]

Religion was therefore entering into competition with these adulthood-oriented, 'moralistic', and 'spiritual', but not religious views of the world.

The Hadow report 1926

The Labour government of 1924, with Sir Charles Trevelyan as President of the Board of Education, appointed a committee under the chairmanship of Sir William Hadow, to look into the education of the working-class adolescent. R.H. Tawney, the prominent Labour intellectual, was a member. The committee is known for its recommendation of secondary education 'for all', not just for middle- and upper-class children. In the 1926 Hadow report the emphasis on religion and the life of the spirit is definitely less than in previous documents. But it still expresses an elevated conception of what adults were undertaking when they put and kept children in schools.

For Hadow the first things in life are *not* those of the spirit. But there are still extremely strong elements of *adult control* of the development of children in their own best interests and the interests of society.

The first great end of the school, Hadow says, is 'the forming and strengthening of *character*—individual and national character—through the placing of youth, in the hours of its growth, "as it were in the fair meadow" of a congenial and inspiring environment'.

Another is the training of boys and girls to delight in pursuits and rejoice in accomplishments—work in music and art; work in wood and metals; work in literature and the record of human history.

And another still is the awakening and guiding of the 'practical intelligence', for the better and more skilled service of the community.[35]

Child-centred Education

But adult-oriented, moralistic and spiritual views of the world were themselves being challenged by rival educational theories. Moralistic educational theories often put the child 'at the centre', but merely as a *tactic* which served the educational purposes of the adult. These rival theories put the child's own judgement and choice genuinely at the centre of school education—the old ideals of Rousseau's

Emile. These theories were also in various ways highly physical and materialistic.

The views of John Dewey, as put forward by him in, for example, *The School and Society* in 1899, underlay a great deal of this new child-centred English thinking.[36] For Dewey, childhood was for the children, and adults should not treat it principally as an ethical preparation for adulthood—certainly not as a religious preparation for eternity. His view is sometimes crudely summarised as 'truth is what works'. Children should be faced with 'practical' concerns, rather than given instruction in traditional subjects. The experience of the child must be 'real'. Learning, in the most famous of Dewey's slogans, must be doing.[37]

Derived from Dewey was much of the experimentation in the 'play way'; influential books such as Percy Nunn's *Education: its data and first principles*; the second Hadow report, and the Spens report.[38]

Dewey's ideas were not new; similar views had already taken root in nineteenth-century England. Wordsworth in *The Prelude* had glorified the power of the undirected experiences of childhood to 'impregnate and to elevate the mind'—at least those experiences unconnected with 'the mean and vulgar works of man'.[39] At the first International Conference on Education, held in London in 1884, Professor Armstrong had already put forward the 'heuristic' or 'discovery' method, insisting that science must be taught as a method of investigation and not as the memorising of an organised system of knowledge.[40]

Sir G.W. Kekewich was appointed Secretary of the Education Department in 1890. His creed was that children came first, 'before everything and everybody'. Among his objectives were the abolition of cramming, the limitation of home lessons and after-school hours, the discouragement of excessive corporal punishment and the encouragement of 'methods of teaching that led the child to good habits and true knowledge through intelligence and interest, instead of driving him by fear and force'.

He was responsible for the 1890 Code that practically ended the Newcastle Commission's system of payment by results. The 1890 Code, he said, was based on two main principlès. The first was to substitute for the bald teaching of facts, and for the cramming that children had to endure in order to pass the annual examination and earn a grant, the development of interest and intelligence and the acquirement of real substantial knowledge. The second was the recognition of the duty of the state to care for the physical welfare of the children. Physical education, sports and games, out-of-doors teaching in fresh air, were therefore all encouraged.[41] Obviously, in this scheme, no one was entitled to force or foist adult religious beliefs onto the growing child.

The Hadow report 1931

The Hadow report of 1931 was concerned with children up to the age of 11 in elementary schools. The leading Labour party intellectual of the time, R.H. Tawney, was an influential member of this Hadow committee, as he had been on the first Hadow committee.

Hadow characterised English working-class education as having passed through three stages since the state first made grants in 1833.

In the first stage, which Hadow clearly implies lasted until about 1870, even some of those who agreed that it was desirable that children should learn to read, 'if only for the best of purposes, that they may read the Scriptures', were doubtful if it was desirable to teach them to write, since 'such a degree of knowledge might produce in them a disrelish for the laborious occupations of life'. No evidence is adduced for this astonishing statement.

Hadow's second stage was the period of the Newcastle Commission's Revised Code and the early School Boards. 'The dominant—and, indeed, it is hardly an exaggeration to say, the exclusive—concern of most schools was to secure that children acquired a minimum standard of proficiency in reading, writing and arithmetic.'

The third stage was dated from about 1890, but especially since 1918. It was a stage in which the outlook of the primary school had been broadened and 'humanised'.

Hadow reported that the elementary school for under-elevens now included physical care through the school medical services. The school offered children 'larger opportunities for physical activity' (in those days there was no sensitivity about a double entendre or any consciousness that there could be one). It handled the curriculum, Hadow said, 'not only as consisting of lessons to be mastered, but as providing fields of new and interesting experience to be explored; it appeals less to passive obedience and more to the sympathy, social spirit and imagination of the children, relies less on mass instruction and more on the encouragement of the individual and group work, and treats the school, in short, not as the antithesis of life, but as its complement and commentary'.

The essential point in any curriculum had to be how to make use of certain elements of experience, because they are part of the common life of mankind. The aim of the school was to introduce its pupils to such experiences in an orderly and intelligent manner, so as to develop their innate powers and to 'awaken them' to the 'basic interests of civilised existence'. The purpose and significance of the school had to be appreciated, 'at least in part', by the children themselves.[42] The curriculum was to be thought of in terms of 'activity and experience' rather than 'the knowledge of acquired facts to be stored'. Its aim should be to develop in the child 'the fundamental human powers' and to awaken him to 'the fundamental interests of civilised life'.[43]

The highly materialistic, though elevated, view of life held by the author or authors of the Hadow report is seen clearly in the emphasis on the physical amenity of the school, not for its *physical* advantages, but for its moral force. It is idle to give lessons on good manners, the report says, if the surroundings of the classroom are unhygienic or mean. 'It should hardly be necessary to insist not only that classrooms must be sunny and airy but that every school should contain ... lavatories with an abundant supply of hot water wherever possible ... and make provision for school meals where necessary.'[44]

1944: Spiritual Development, Collective Worship and Agreed Religious Instruction

In spite of all the confident and considerable advances made in conferences, national reports, local bureaucracies, training colleges and the schools by exponents of materialistic causation, humanistic virtue and child-centred education, when these matters came before Parliament the 'progressive' educational politicians, academics, administrators and teachers lost out to what was to them religious and educational reaction.

In 1938 the National Society published Phyllis Dent's book on religious education. Too much attention was being paid, she said, to the institutional arrangements between the Church of England and the state. It was time to return to a consideration of what 'religious education' should be, in content and method. It had to be founded *unambiguously* on *Christian* conviction.[45]

The Church of England at the highest level was determined to make its distinctive contribution in the wholly state schools. William Temple, though his reign was very short (1942-44), is sometimes spoken of as the greatest Archbishop of Canterbury since St Anselm. He was certainly the most influential Church of England educational figure in the early 1940s. He insisted that the Church of England had to say 'what it is about' the current state-Church arrangements for school education that '*we* believe in'. The Church of England had to be satisfied that the arrangements '*can* be delivered by the *dual* system *and in no other way*'. '*All* true education', Temple wrote, in terms no less firm than his mediaeval predecessors, 'must be religious in its basis and texture.'[46] The issue, for him, was the nature of Christian education in the state school, as well as in the Church of England school.

Temple, when he was still Archbishop of York, stated his views about the relation between the Church of England and the state school in his *Citizen and Churchman*.

The *primary* duty of the state, he wrote, 'is to maintain that order which makes possible the free and unimpeded activity of its citizens'.

The state is entrusted with force in order that it may prevent the use of force by anyone else; if its own force is known to be sufficient, no one will resort to force from anger, ambition, or any other personal motive. In fact it may be truly said that the state is entrusted with force in the hope that, as a result, there will be no use of force within the community at all, except such disciplinary use of it in the subordinate communities (families, schools, etc.) as illustrates in its own sphere the same principle—force as the instrument of law.[47]

But having come into existence to make life safe, the state extends its activities in the interest of 'welfare', 'including the moral welfare of its citizens'.[48] The state, then, is a servant of God 'for the preservation of justice and for the promotion of human welfare so far as this can be done by universal enactment'.

In addition to its moral function, the state has a 'spiritual function'. But the spiritual function of the state cannot be rightly exercised directly by Acts of Uniformity and the like. Its spiritual function is 'not to regulate religion but to make free scope for it and uphold the regulations made for its expression *by the religious associations* themselves'.[49]

Church of England Christianity is not just a belief in Christianity, or in 'religion', or in 'God'. Though there are many denominations and other faiths that contain large elements of the truth, the Church of England comes closest to understanding and expressing the meaning of Christianity in its fullest sense.

The Church of England, Temple says, believes that men have pursued a self-centred existence, each following his own will in preference to God's.[50] The *original sin* of man is his *self-centredness*. This shows itself in 'each setting up his will in the place of God's'.

Each man, making himself the centre of his own view and estimate of the world, thinks of God (if at all) as only one of the beings who impinges on his existence, and of other men as deriving their importance from their relations to himself.[51]

Religious beliefs are not an inert adjunct to mundane existence. Christianity, and the Church of England's (and any other sect's or denomination's) beliefs about Christianity, have their own powerful consequences for the individual and society. In the Church of England view, sins have been committed by the 'vitiated race' of self-centred men, Temple says, and self-centred men have piled a 'burden of evil' on themselves and others.

Within any society or organisation, of course, there were people who led more selfish, and people who led less selfish lives. Which of them had the upper hand in public opinion and public life also had consequences. While recognising the needs for reform that new times imposed, for generations the Book of Common Prayer had warned against people who were simply 'given to change', and who always had 'a greater regard to their own private fancies and interests, than to that duty they owe to the public'.[52]

The religious requirements imposed on state schools by the Education Act 1944

Temple discussed the religious clauses of the 1944 Education Act with the President of the Board of Education, R.A. Butler, much of the spadework having been undertaken by the general secretary of the National Society, Canon E.F. Hall.

In the parliamentary debate on the new legal requirement, that there must be an act of collective worship in state schools, some opposition was expressed. Some MPs, while approving the fact that the act of collective worship did take place already in nearly all state schools, objected to it now being made compulsory. The freedom of both teacher and pupil would be infringed by the requirement.[53] An act of worship was an interior thing that could not be enforced by an external authority.[54]

Butler replied that although it would now for the first time be compulsory for the school staff to arrange a collective act of worship, the conscience clause removed all compulsion from the individual child to engage in it.[55]

An amendment against the legal requirement that there should be a collective act of worship in state schools was defeated by 121 votes to 20.

In the debate on the provision for compulsory religious instruction the main point made in the debate was, however, that the syllabus would be *too weak*. 'I would rather have the religion that is envisaged in this clause than no religion at all', one speaker protested, but the feeble provisions as they stood were 'not going to help the cause of religion.'[56] Another speaker said that the very existence of a free state depends upon the general acceptance of the *Christian* belief that *'as a soul precious in the sight of God'* every individual must be treated with equal dignity.[57]

Of the 31 speeches on the Bill in the House of Commons, 20 were largely concerned with the religious issue, and 224 members of the Lords and Commons signed a declaration calling for a strengthening of worship and religious instruction in schools.

The results were satisfactory to all the parties to these discussions. The 1944 Education Act required every local authority to contribute to the 'spiritual, moral, mental and physical' development (listed in that order) of the population of its area.[58]

Religious 'education' was to be provided through 'worship' and 'instruction'. The school day in every state-supported voluntary school and every state school had to begin with a collective act of worship. Religious instruction was to be given in every state-supported voluntary and every state school. In every state school religious instruction had to be given in accordance with the provisions of an locally-agreed syllabus.[59] Attendance at worship or instruction could be excused on grounds of conscience, thus carrying on the tradition of the Cowper-Temple clause of the 1870 Act.

The concept of an agreed syllabus for religious instruction had been used on an ad hoc basis in a few counties since 1924. The 1944 Act gave it legal force. Each local authority was made responsible for drawing up its own agreed syllabus. The agreed syllabus was to be the work of four committees.

1. A committee of representatives of any 'religious denominations' (*sic* not 'Christian denominations') that the *local authority* considered should be present;

2. In England, a committee of representatives of the Church of England;

3. A committee of representatives of teachers; and

4. A committee of representatives of the local authority. Each committee had one vote, and the religious syllabus had to secure all four votes. Any one of the committees, therefore had a veto on any religious syllabus that was proposed.

The Act refers only to 'religious' worship and 'religious' instruction. *Christian* worship and instruction was not specified. But Chuter-Ede, the Labour parliamentary secretary to the President of the Board of Education, R.A. Butler, and a typical representative of the strong contingents of old-fashioned 'chapel and temperance' socialism in the Labour party, said that there was a general recognition that, whatever the parents' own faith or lack of it, they wanted their children to have a grounding in the 'principles of the *Christian* faith', as it *'ought to be practised in this country'*.[60] A government spokesman in the House of Lords, the Earl of Selborne, had already given strong assurances that the intention of the government, and the intention of Parliament, was that 'the syllabus teaching to be given should be *Christian* teaching, and that the worship should be *Christian* worship'.[61]

Christianity was not specified, not because there was any doubt about the education being Christian, but for the opposite reason. Parliament feared that a Christian denomination might object in the courts that a particular syllabus was not Christian enough. Let sleeping dogs lie. 'What "undenominational teaching" is, is a matter which by now is well understood in this country.'[62]

The Bishop of Chichester nevertheless pointed out at the time that, all that being granted, the omission of the word 'Christian' could prove to be significant in the future, because the assurances of ministers of the crown had no force in law.[63]

The early agreed syllabuses

Religious instruction in the state schools was thus to be given in accordance with locally-agreed syllabuses, to be unanimously agreed by four committees. One of these committees would represent the Church of England, one would represent other 'religious denominations' in the area, one the local authority, and the fourth, the teachers. The state-supported voluntary schools, including the Church of England schools, were given power to draw up their own schemes.

Many of the locally-agreed syllabuses that had been drawn up unofficially during the period between the two world wars and were revised when the school leaving age was raised to 15.

Until the early 1960s the locally-agreed syllabuses were entirely Christian. Characteristically they started with the Bible and left the teacher to build up Christian teaching on this basis.[64]

The Student Christian Movement (SCM) became active in the schools to reverse this procedure. The SCM scheme began with 'problems' that were 'modern'; from them pupils were to be led back to the Bible. The West Riding Syllabus of Religious Instruction of 1947 was a typical product of SCM influence. In dealing with modern problems, the syllabus laid down, the teacher should endeavour to develop in the pupil certain 'essential attitudes of thought'. The pupil was to 'think honestly and sincerely, but to treat with respect the opinions of those who differ from him *if* they are also sincere and honest in their thought'. The pupil was to preserve an open mind, not rejecting any point of view simply because it is new. But neither should the pupil 'rashly adopt' any point of view simply *because* it was new.

The kind of 'personal and moral' modern problem that should be considered by the pupil was why it was wrong to swear; why it is wrong to eat or drink or smoke (*sic*) 'too much'; why it is wrong to speak (or even think) 'impurely' about sex. It was still taken for granted in the state schools as well as the Church of England schools, that is, that it *was* plainly 'wrong' to do any of these things; the question was why it was wrong.

The list of modern problems provided was 'the use of atomic weapons, war, slums, gambling, unemployment, sharp practice in business, observance of Sunday, propaganda, scandal, sex, and divorce'.

In considering such modern 'social' problems, what should be 'the *Christian's* attitude'? The pupil was to apply the 'knowledge and experience' he already had about the nature of God and the example of Jesus Christ. He was then to make 'his personal decision' to live up to Christ's example.[65]

Mark Chater calls this sort of religious education, the sort that is concerned with transmitting the beliefs and morals of Christianity, the 'confessional approach'—the Christian faith taught as true. It was the approach taken, he writes, 'universally by the voluntary and the county schools in the maintained sector up until the 1960s, as agreed syllabuses and examination courses from the 1930s onwards show'.[66] 'This approach was Bible-based, assumed the existence of a mono-cultural Christian society and, usually, expected that most of the population would attend major Christian festivals like Christmas and Easter.' The intention, though less explicit than it was in the Church of England schools, was to help children in the state schools, too, to grow in the Christian faith.[67]

The 1960s: Losing Ground

As early as 1953 there were signs that the influence of the Church of England on state-school religious education was waning. In that year the National Society's policy statement said that it regarded 'the content of religious education as a primary concern'. In that connection, the National Society felt it necessary to record that it 'maintained the right' to 'express views'. That the National Society should feel it necessary to say this, as the first point of its five-point policy statement, was perhaps an indication of its sense of losing ground to other contenders for influence over the character of state schools *and of the state-subsidised Church of England schools*.[68] As everyone, from the lowest to highest in the land, had and still has that abstract 'right' to express views, it seems likely that it was its polite way of saying that it should continue to be *in a position to exert effective influence where it counted*.

The Newsom report

In 1963 the members of the Newsom committee devoted a chapter of their report to 'spiritual and moral development'. 'Religious instruction in accordance with *any* local authority's agreed syllabus', the report said, 'is *instruction* in the *Christian* religion.' In some respects the report itself still upheld what it called 'the traditional standards of this country which are based on the Christian way of life'. In particular, in the Christian way of life sexual morality was 'based on chastity before marriage and fidelity within it'.

But the teacher was not asked to 'teach' Christian morality or any Christian beliefs. The teacher was to 'endeavour' to bring about moral and religious results. He or she should simply 'present' the Christian values, and—a contradiction in terms?—'offer' pupils 'firm guidance'.

But the report took for granted that Christianity was to be in *some sense* 'taught'. 'A teacher must know the Bible, and *its* teaching.' 'His scholarship must be up to date.' He must move on 'the frontiers of today', but these are described as the '*Christian* frontiers'.[69]

The Church of England hierarchy

Yet the Church of England's teaching at the highest levels of its own hierarchy and in its own leading educational circles was soon to move in the direction of agreement with intelligent and influential secular opinion on the subject of what was viable, religiously and morally, in its 'Christianity'.

Throughout the 1960s Robert Runcie, who was to be Archbishop of Canterbury throughout the 1980s, was Principal of Cuddesdon, a theological college that produced many bishops. In a taped interview he summed up the Cuddesdon ethos as 'detached, slightly amused liberalism'; Cuddesdon was 'sophisticated'.[70] When in March 1963 John Robinson, Bishop of Woolwich, published his short book, *Honest to God*, questioning the conception of the deity hitherto propagated as Christian, Runcie remembers Hugh Montefiore saying to him, 'My God, John Robinson's written a book which is going to cause mayhem—he's going to tell the world the sort of things *we* believe!' David Jenkins (later to be Bishop of Durham) was lecturing all this radical stuff to his students, Runcie said, 'so it wouldn't be a big problem to them'.[71]

Religious education in Church of England schools

At the beginning of the 1970s the National Society expressed its full satisfaction with the recommendations of the then Bishop of Durham's report on the future of religious education. The Durham report changed the balance of religious education for the next 25 or 30 years: away from inculcating the principles of the Church of England; away from introducing pupils principally to Christianity; and towards the 'study' of 'religions' in the plural, and bodies of thought resembling religions.

The National Society announced that in future its official writing paper should cease to give equal emphasis to all the elements of its title. In future prominence was to be given to 'promoting religious education'. 'According to the principles of the Church of England' would still appear, but less conspicuously.[72] In 1972 its Charter was revised 'to secure a flexibility appropriate to the circumstances of the day'.[73]

Noel Todd, a former head teacher of a Church of England primary school, documents what he sees as the drift of the National Society from then on towards a secular position on education in its own schools.[74] The Manchester diocesan syllabus of 1994 permitted Christianity to be studied for only 50 per cent of the time. *Church of England* schools in the diocese were encouraged to follow the Church's national guidelines for the *state* schools.[75]

The New Forms of Religious Education in State Schools after 1970

In the 1970s the agreed syllabuses began to be questioned and then rejected within many state schools *and within some voluntary schools*.

Richmansworth

Dr Mark Chater, of Bishop Grosseteste University College, Lincoln, lists seven factors that caused this.[76] His own analysis constitutes in itself, in its assumptions, language and authorities, an excellent example of the view of the world and religion that prevailed after 1970.

1. There was a theological revolution in Britain in the 1960s, symbolised by *Honest to God*.

2. There was a growing consensus that Britain, from the late fifties onwards, became a plural or pluralist society. The distinction Chater is making between 'plural' and 'pluralist' is not clear. This change was partly brought by the appearance of non-Christian communities whose worship and life-style did not fit the pattern that had been tacitly accepted prior to that date. Such changes continued to be recognised and celebrated in official reports (for instance the Swann report of 1985).[77]

3. The introduction of comprehensive schools affected the curricula that children were able to follow. Previously children selected for educational ability who attended grammar schools were able to pass public examinations. The advent of mixed-ability teaching and larger schools entailed the scrutinisation (*sic*) of established curricula.

4. The work of Ronald Goldman and Ken Hyde questioned the usefulness of entirely Bible-based religious education. Goldman considered that proper understanding of the Bible required children to think abstractly, and that this ability was not possessed by the majority of primary school children or by many at secondary school.[78] Hyde considered that children failed to learn Christian materials without the support of church attendance. As church attendance had diminished, the curriculum had to be changed.[79]

5. Since education involves the induction of pupils into 'autonomous' bodies of knowledge, it was illogical to speak of a 'Christian' education in any meaningful sense. There was therefore a growing demand by secularists for a re-focusing of religious education.[80] (Among Chater's

references to *secularist* demands is the Bishop of Durham's report of 1970 to the National Society.)

6. The tendency to nationalise the curriculum. Before the National Curriculum, the curricula in schools tended to be regionally flavoured. Large-scale national curriculum 'model' projects of the new type were developed. They were taken up as 'safe' by some LEAs, even though there was no legal requirement for them to do so. The Schools Council, in some of it projects and working papers, recommended new approaches to religion in the classroom, and rejected the so-called 'confessional' approach as inappropriate to state schools.[81]

7. Individual attacks on the confessional approach. Those who wrote on religious education all (*sic*) recommended changes to, or the abandonment of, a confessional approach and devised new schemes of work to fit the new educational scene and pluralist climate.[82]

The Christianity of the agreed syllabuses of the 1950s and 1960s was therefore, Chater says, 'considered inappropriate for publicly-funded education'. Church of England schools were also, of course, now heavily 'publicly funded'.

Post-1960s' Church of England morality

The theology of the 1960s at the highest level was followed by the morality of the 1970s and early 1980s at the highest level, both being distinguished by their tendency to assimilate themselves to current secular thinking.

Clifford Longley recalls a seminar he attended in 1982, organised by the British Council of Churches. 'The usual suspects were there, bishops and archdeacons, professors of theology, chairmen of church committees, plus a sprinkling of outsiders.' One of the outsiders was a senior police officer from Scotland Yard. What struck Longley was the fact that the policeman believed that given average unsaintly human nature and the ethics of the modern world, if people were not controlled by internalised beliefs in their duty to God and their neighbour, no amount of policing could combat the ensuing volume of selfish crime. By contrast, the bishops and archdeacons viewed the problem of human nature and the view that crime had risen with 'soporific liberal optimism', and regarded social control as no business of religion.

What those senior clergymen in 1982 completely lacked, Longley said, was any foreboding that the marginalisation of the beliefs and traditions their predecessors had stood for, was likely in the long run to do great damage to the loose-knit society of emancipated individuals they so admired.[83]

The school study of 'world religions'

In 1977 the Commission for Racial Equality published *The Shap Handbook on World Religions in Education*. This was the work of the so-called Shap working party, a group whose purpose was to foster the study of world religions in schools by, among other things, organising in-service training for teachers.[84]

Professor Ninian Smart popularised the school study of world religions.[85] The study of world religions, according to a supporter, provided a 'new, more objective, and therefore more academically respectable' justification for a subject that had been 'discredited and weakened' by the 'collapse' of 1950s' style agreed syllabuses and common worship.[86]

Smart shaped two landmark documents. One was the Schools Council's *Religious Education in Secondary Schools*. In the neutral, open study of different religions the pupil is faced with the task of 'penetrating to the heart and mind of the believer'. This, for Smart, was a scientific, but also an 'empathetic' process.

In the 1980s more than half of the local education authorities adopted new locally-agreed syllabuses. Rachel Tingle studied them and concluded that nearly all of them had adopted a world religions or multi-faith approach.[87]

Given the relativistic slant of the study of world religions in the schools, it is well to note here that to empathise means to see what other people see, to feel what other people feel. It is possible for a sensitive person, if he or she takes the time and trouble, to be able to see what somebody else believes to be the facts of the situation and appreciate why, in emotional or moral terms, he or she then reacts to the situation, as he or she has defined it. But the results of that empathy is not necessarily sympathy. Still less is it necessarily agreement. The fact that one understands another person's conduct and point of view has very little to do with the question of either the factual correctness or the emotional appropriateness or the moral or religious validity of that person's conduct and point of view (or, of course, of one's own).

The other landmark document was the Birmingham Agreed Syllabus of 1975. The Birmingham Agreed Syllabus included 'Communism' and 'Humanism' as 'life-stances' to be studied by secondary pupils in religious education.'[88] 'Smart's development of phenomenology made it accessible to school-based religious education.'[89] (What 'phenomenology' was in this context is discussed in another chapter.)

Locally-agreed syllabuses by the mid-1980s ranged from those of West Sussex, whose 1983 syllabus gave 'a clear lead in the prime importance in our country of Christian belief, values and heritage', and gave 'no more than an introduction' to other faiths,[90] to the Brent locally-agreed syllabus of 1985, which studied 'faiths', but said that the word 'faith' was to be understood to mean 'any consistent, coherent and ethical life-stance whether theistic or non-theistic'.[91]

The 1944 Act's references to the committee composed of 'other denominations than the Church of England'—one of the four committees that decided the locally-agreed syllabuses—were not repealed. 'Other denominations than the Church of England' was informally reinterpreted so as to include 'other faiths and secular viewpoints than Christianity'.

By the mid-1980s, courses leading to the award of the General Certificate of Education (GCSE) in Religious Studies had to be based on the study of one, two or three of the major world religions; at least one syllabus had to be concerned wholly with the study of Christianity. Given the available choices, a number of the courses offered by the GCSE examining boards could be followed without studying

Christianity at all. In the study of Christianity the trend was away from a study of the Bible, and in Religious Studies the trend was towards personal responses to world-faith 'themes' in the style of 'which marriage rite *appeals* to *you*?'

Religious education was no longer what it had been for centuries, namely, Christianity that claimed the right to suffuse the whole life of the school. It was no longer the non-sectarian study of Christianity as a faith to be accepted. It was no longer Christianity taught according to an agreed syllabus, within the context of a daily act of normally Christian worship in the school. Religion was a secular school subject like any other. All traces of Christian, not just Church of England, 'indoctrination' had to be expunged. In many schools religious education paid no special attention to Christianity at all.

Revival and Resistance

Revival

Though expressions of disquiet with the content of post-1970s' religious teaching in Church and state schools were rare, they were never quite stilled. In his 1978 Reith lectures, Edward Norman, at that time Dean of Peterhouse, Cambridge, drew attention to what he saw as the 'marked similarity' between the typical school course on religion in the Soviet Union and the new courses in Britain. In the Soviet Union the courses were deliberately aimed at fostering 'scientific atheism' as an essential component of communism. In Britain they were being pressed on the schools by *Christian* educational theorists whose political amateurism and social utopianism unwittingly made them easy targets for the enemies of Christianity.[92]

In the late-1980s and the 1990s there was a revival in some quarters of the view that the Christianity of the historic Church of England was the God-given basis for a life led on this earth—and therefore worthy of being taught in the state schools of the country, always with the right of dissenters, religious, political or philosophical, to exclude their children from such education.

In 1994 the Anglican Bishop of Guildford, the Roman Catholic Bishop of Leeds, Rabbi Dr Julian Jacobs, the secretary of the Division of Social Responsibility of the Methodist Church, the convenor of the Church of Scotland's Board of Social Responsibility, and the head of a university Department of Religious Studies collaborated in trying to answer the question, 'Teaching Right and Wrong: have the churches failed?'[93]

In the opinion of the Anglican head of the Department of Religious Studies, 'the only institution capable of teaching religion is a church, the only personnel capable of teaching religion are properly qualified ... practising members of the faith in question—Reverends, Rabbis, Imams'. So far as Christianity in this country was concerned, he wrote, the post-modernist atmosphere of social and religious studies and cognate subjects in schools had reduced the matter to absurdity. It was as if a teacher of zoology or botany were to be appointed and approved, he wrote, who thought that there was no difference between a banana and a kangaroo; or that it was only a matter of opinion as to how they were to be distinguished; and if they were different, that it was a matter of small importance.[94]

Edward Norman, as Chancellor of York Minster, complained that, in the late-twentieth century, Muslim, Hindu, Buddhist and other beliefs and practices had been 'safely sanitised' by the schools, to avoid giving offence to ethnic minorities. Christianity, by contrast, had been presented as a mass of criticisms for its espousal of now proven errors, for its cultural insensitivity, and for its backwardness in political and social policy. The schools were not passing on Christianity to posterity. 'Nor, evidently, were the Churches.'[95]

The religious education provisions of the 1988 Act

The National Society played a major role in strengthening the position of religious education in the 1988 Education Reform Bill. The House of Lords agreed on 3 May 1988, with government support, that religious education was to be part of the basic curriculum; that the 'agreed syllabus' system was to be confirmed and strengthened; and that every local education authority had to set up a standing advisory committee on religious education (SACRE).

Caroline Cox, Baroness Cox, had become concerned with the character and effects of the types of religious education in schools that had emerged in the three decades since the 1944 Act, and especially since 1970. That children in ways suited to their age should receive an education in the principal world religions was, she believed, beyond question desirable. The principal world faiths, like all other powerful and widespread conceptions of the natural world and supernatural forces, including atheism, had been and were *important* in their *different* personal and social effects, dire or beneficent from person to person, place to place, and time to time. Her principal objection was to children being invited to approach world religions with the mind-set that different faiths (and perhaps no faith) were somehow 'all the same'.

What was objectionable, too, was the indiscriminate admixture of the religions that had had a major impact on large populations over extended periods of history with modern fads or exotic rites taken out of their cultural context. She referred to a book widely used in religious education in schools in the 1980s, *Beginning Religion*.[96] The earlier edition, she protested, suggested children could go to a séance as part of their homework. There were ouija boards. There was a picture of human sacrifice, all rather cartoon-like. The Lord's Prayer was dealt with on the same page as shamanism. A letter had been sent to Inner London Education Authority heads by the RE inspectors saying that parents had complained about their children becoming psychologically disturbed by teaching on the occult. Representations were made against a school in York that had spent the whole summer teaching witchcraft and had visited witches covens.[97]

When the 1988 Educational Reform Bill came from the Commons, Baroness Cox suggested an amendment to the Bishop who had special responsibility for education in the Lords, the Bishop of London. The amendment would recognise that Britain was now a society in which other faiths were now represented, but would require religious education in all maintained schools to be 'predominantly' Christian education. Parents from other faiths would have the right to withdraw their children, so that they could receive their own religious education and take part in worship in their own faith.

The Bishop of London said that he did not wish to put the amendment, 'because it would divide the College of Bishops'.[98] Baroness Cox said that in that case she would put it herself.

In the debate her amendment was supported by the Chief Rabbi, Lord Jacobovits, who derided what he called the 'cocktail of world faiths'. If Christianity suffers, he said, 'so does every other faith'. Viscount Buckmaster, claiming to speak for the country's Muslims, said that they felt strongly that 'Christian education in the schools should be given a more positive image'. Baroness Cox told the House that the Imam of one of London's leading mosques had recently led two or three thousand Muslims in prayer that the name of Christ would once again be revered in Britain's schools.

Looking straight at the Bishop's bench, Baroness Cox added, 'Would that our bishops could be heard praying the same prayer'.[99] 'Woe to you, Prelates! Ye have no skill to teach ... '[100]

Clifford Longley, the senior press commentator on religious affairs, contributed an article to *The Times* on the Bill.[101] There were two issues, one secular, the other religious. On the secular point, a generation had grown up, he wrote, that had little or no knowledge of Christianity. Self-induced amnesia cannot be good for a society; the role of Christianity had been crucial in the shaping of this country's history. On the religious point, religious education as it was now taught gave pupils little grasp of either Christianity or any other religion. They were left with an educational mish-mash. By treating all religions as equally suitable for the child, the effect of religious education since 1970 had been to have them all dismissed as being of no practical importance. Nine bishops wrote a letter to *The Times* supporting him.[102]

The same two points, the one secular, the other religious, were made in the House of Commons. Alan Beith, a Methodist, said that an understanding of religion, especially the Christian religion, was essential for 'understanding the society, history and heritage of these islands'.[103] Timothy Raison said that it was 'wholly impossible to understand British culture without knowledge of the Bible and the Book of Common Prayer'.[104] Kenneth Baker, replying for the government, made the same secular case for teaching Christianity. He agreed that 'a fundamental part' of any religious education syllabus should be the *Christian* faith. Religious education, he said, should involve exposing children to 'the possibility of belief' and 'the experience of faith'. The teaching of 'spiritual values' should 'imbue the whole curriculum'. Christianity should be taught for secular reasons, because it had 'woven its way through our history'.[105]

Religious instruction solely for religious reasons was pressed by Sir Rhodes Boyson, who said that there must be *faith*. *Such* religious education had to be a core subject, 'and the churches ... must ensure that it is taught'.[106]

The Bishop of London finally agreed to take the issue forward. He would consult all the interested parties, and he would then himself move the amendment.[107] He was chairman of the National Society, and it was in the National Society's offices that the wording was worked out that became Section 8 (3) of the 1988 Act.

The 1988 Act was intended to promote the 'spiritual, moral, cultural, mental and physical development of pupils' and to prepare them 'for the opportunities, responsibilities and experiences of adult life'.[108]

Worship in voluntary schools was to be determined in accordance with the school's trust deed, or its practice before 1944, by its governors after consultation with the head teacher.

The Act required that, in future, agreed syllabuses for the state schools must 'reflect the fact that the religious traditions of Great Britain are in the main Christian', and that daily worship in schools should be 'normally' Christian.[109]

The 1944 Act had given discretionary powers to local education authorities to set up SACREs—the four committees, each having a vote. The 'other denominations' committee was renamed 'Christian and other denominations'. This wording retrospectively exonerated local authorities who had for long been stretching the meaning of 'other denominations' to include also 'other faiths'.[110] The 1988 Act required local authorities to set up SACREs. A syllabus conference would then draw up the agreed syllabus.

Parents were entitled to withdraw their children wholly or in part from religious education or religious worship.[111] If the parents wanted their children to receive religious education of a kind not provided by the school, they could be withdrawn from school for such time as was 'reasonably necessary' for this kind of education to be given. Where most children were not Christian, they could have an act of worship and religious instruction in their own faith, while a separate act of worship and religious education would be provided for the Christian children. In a school where there was a minority of children from another faith, an application could be made to the SACREs for permission for them to have their own act of worship.[112]

The Cowper-Temple clause was abolished: an amendment to the Bill made it clear that wholly state schools *were* now allowed to deal with the catechisms and formularies of different denominations—so long as pupils were not given the impression that they were true. State schools could not *teach* distinctive religious beliefs, but they could *study* such beliefs.[113]

These matters were dealt with officially in DES Circular 1/89, which made it clear that by law 'religious education has equal standing in relation to the core and foundation subjects within a school's curriculum'.[114]

The General Synod

The General Synod expressed the reaction *in its own voluntary sector* towards the traditional beliefs of the Church of England in school education in, for example, the declaration in 1998 on the distinctiveness of Church of

England schools. This declaration led the Board of Education to issue an 'ethos statement' that was widely adopted.
It stated that education in Church of England schools must
be 'bold and decisive'. The faith should not be imposed, but
Christ is to there to be 'offered as a gift to be experienced'.
The Church of England school derived its ethos from, and
took its stand on, 'the love of God and the commandment to
love your neighbour'.

Relativism, the statement said, has flourished for
decades. It was now entrenched in much of academic and
public discourse. As a result, all shared systems of values
had been undermined. The Church of England, by contrast,
offered 'a sure foundation for personal and social values',
based on the person and ministry of Christ.

The Church of England school, with this ethos, embodied
in its everyday life 'the Christian understanding of the
world'. It encourages, confidently, an understanding of the
meaning and significance of the Christian faith and 'pro-
motes Christian values through the experience it offers all
its pupils'.[115]

At the end of the year 2000 Lord Dearing's review group
formulated the Church of England's 'mission to the nation'
in a few brief statements:

> We see this as to proclaim the Gospel, to nourish Christians in
> their faith, to bring others to the faith, and the nurture and
> maintenance of the dignity of the image of God in human beings
> through service, speaking out on important issues and work for
> social justice.[116]

Church schools, the review group said, were places where
this faith was to be 'proclaimed and lived'. In an increasingly secular society the Church of England was right, it
said, to respond to the concern of Christian parents to give
their children the opportunity to experience what it was to
learn in a distinctively Christian environment.[117]

The government's educational proposals, February 2001

These pluralistic ideas, in the pre-1970 sense of pluralistic—strong groups taking strong positions, in contrast to a
mass of individuals 'tolerating' everything and taking
responsibility for nothing—appeared in the educational

Nothing about Croxley

proposals put forward by the government at the beginning of the year 2001. Both the prime minister, Tony Blair, and the secretary of state for education, David Blunkett, stressed the need to develop a system where every school had its own mission and ethos. Schools were to be encouraged to develop their own admissions policies. So far as resources would allow—a constraint on all policies—parents would be free to send their children to the distinctive school of their choice (within the limits of what their children themselves would want, would allow or could resist).[118]

It remains to be seen whether or to what extent so large a role for the state is compatible with the independence of organisations—whether what might be called 'the nationalisation of pluralism', pursued also in proposals for everything from state-financed political parties to state-aid for the humblest voluntary play group, is a sociological possibility or, on the contrary, a political chimera.

The Dearing Report, June 2001

Lord Dearing's review group reported in June 2001.[119] Dearing welcomed the fact that the keen inter-denominational rivalries of the past were no longer an issue in school provision. An ecumenical approach therefore could mean drawing on the resources of two or more denominations in turning an existing school into a Christian school. But it also meant, in particular, *respect* for other denominational schools. The ecumenical aim here must not be to weaken denominational distinctiveness, Dearing said. On the contrary, it was to honour the peculiar interests of other denominations, and to avoid 'destabilising' their existing educational provisions.[120]

Dearing rejected the argument that 'secularism' was necessarily 'inclusive', and that a denominational religious education was by its nature divisive. In fact, he said, existing Church of England schools had a very widespread appeal to all sections of society, including to parents not only from other denominations but from other faiths, simply because the schools took faith *seriously*. In principle, 'a Christian understanding of the world' celebrated 'the individuality and equal value of all humanity'.[121]

Dearing therefore recommended that, roughly within the period 2001-2010, the Church of England should increase the number of its secondary school places by the equivalent of 100 schools. These and the Church's existing schools should all have head teachers committed to maintaining the schools' Christian character. Each school would engage 'meaningfully' in a 'real' act of Christian worship every day. The life of the school would incorporate the values of the Christian faith. The school would convey knowledge to its pupils of, among other Christian things, the liturgy of the Church of England (especially Holy Communion), and maintain an 'active and affirming' relationship with the Church of England parish church.[122]

Dearing provided a model 'ethos statement' for all Church of England schools. According to this ethos statement, the purpose of each school was to preserve and develop its character in accordance with the religious principles of the Church of England.

The school's purpose was nevertheless inclusively to 'serve the community' by providing education of the highest quality, to as many as wanted it, and could be accommodated while preserving the school's ethos of Christian belief and practice. Through the 'experiences' that it 'offered', such a school encouraged an understanding of faith, and promoted Christian values.[123]

Resistance

Hostile comment on any form of state-school 'Christianity'

The state-school religious provisions of the 1988 Act met with resistance from the proponents of the new multi-faith, phenomenological and experiential forms of religious education.

The National Society published a leaflet that distanced the Society from the preferential treatment in the state schools (not the Church schools) of Christianity as a religion to be embraced as a religion rather than as an everyday object of academic curiosity. The leaflet also sought to distance the Society from the intention of the Act to see that state-school teaching was *not* neutral on Christianity as compared with other faiths and political or philosophical doctrines.

The leaflet emphasised the purely temporal importance of knowing about 'Christianity and its social implications'. Knowledge about Christianity was necessary, the leaflet said, 'quite apart from any claims about the saving truth of the Gospel which the Church would seek to uphold in the context of its own sphere of activity'.[124]

Other examples from the arguments put by a large variety of opponents are outlined below.

Lord Houghton criticised the religious education amendments of the 1988 Act as 'more of a crusade of moral rearmament'. He warned of 'indoctrination'. The preference given to Christianity by the 1988 Act was like a 'hostile takeover suitable for reference to the Monopolies and Mergers Commission'.[125]

Writers in the broadsheet press continued to assert that Christianity was being imposed on 'every single school child of whatever faith, political persuasion or cultural background'. Where the law, 'not surprisingly', was being ignored, 'fundamentalist thought-police' were noting and reporting the fact.[126]

In November 1988 the journal *Education* deplored the fact that the government had succumbed to the influence of the Church of England. The result was that religious education was still under the control of the faith communities rather than professional educators. The legislators had revealed their ignorance about the aim and purpose of religious education. They simply did not know how it was actually taught in the vast majority of schools in the late 1980s.

In tones of distaste and contempt, the anonymous writer says that the legislators' erroneous view of religious education was that it was 'essentially about religious teaching or religious instruction with all the overtones of confessional approaches, teaching morality etc.'[127]

According to the author of the article, the Bishop of London and the religious education professionals had been on the side of common sense and educational considerations. Opposed to common sense and educational considerations had been the Thatcher government and Lady Cox. The *Christian* churches in particular, the article complains, had control over religious education in schools, though other religious communities were not blameless. 'It will take a great struggle for the professional teachers of religious education to wrest that control away so that it lies within the educational domain.'[128]

Depressing as all that was, the author says, a careful study of the Act gives hope to those who reject the idea of religious education as induction into a faith. There was a 'world of daylight' (*sic*) between the Bishop of London's amendments—the 'educationist' Bishop of London, Graham Leonard—and those of Lady Cox. 'Only careless and over-simplified press reporting' had granted her, and not him, the victory, and had 'offered little comfort to the religious education profession'. Yet, the article argued, the Bishop of London had won, and not Baroness Cox, for Leonard's form of words required a new syllabus only to *'reflect'* the place of Christianity in Great Britain. It had more strongly to *'take account'* of other principal religions. While some religious education specialists might object to having the word 'Christianity' in the Act at all, the author says, the statement does little more than describe the current situation in most agreed syllabuses. It does not say that Christianity should form the bulk of the teaching, be central to it, or be emphasised in it.

The article sounds the optimistic note that the Act, by referring to 'Great Britain', thus legally requires *all* LEAs to teach *'other* principal religions'. It was no longer legally possible to facilitate the study of Islam in Bradford, but miss it off the syllabus in Truro. Future locally-agreed syllabuses 'cannot close their eyes (*sic*) to the plurality of the religious traditions in Britain and plead tunnel vision' (*sic*).[129]

John Hull, the editor of *Learning for Living* from 1971 to 1996, was an influential figure in post-1970s religious education in schools.[130] As Professor of Religious Education at the University of Birmingham he worked in a city in which, by the end of the century, 41 per cent of the school-children were non-white.[131]

Hull welcomed the fact that the 1988 Act placed greater legal emphasis on *religious* education. As a Bill it had had only two lines on religious education. But he deplored Baroness Cox's success in securing preferential treatment for *Christianity*. In his view, the absence of 'Christianity' as a named religion in law from 1870 to 1988 had meant that teachers had been able to 'launch the unique British experience of *multi-faith dialogue* in the classroom' in state schools. This 'enlightened policy' had won worldwide admiration. Now the 'Christianising amendments' of the 1988 Act, he wrote, had overthrown all the progress of the previous 20 or 25 years. 'Christian supremacy' had been imposed through legislation. The Christian provisions of the Act were not conducive to the creation of a multi-cultural Britain.[132]

The following year Professor Hull took a more favourable line when, as he said, he 'unpacked' the Act. But the change seems to have occurred because he now saw in the Act a strengthening of multi-faith education. The Act had made it *compulsory* in *all parts* of the country. The significant thing to note, he said, was 'that it will no longer be possible for parts of the country which are predominantly Christian, or where there are no significant groups of religious adherents other than Christian, to claim that therefore the locally-agreed syllabus should exclude the other principal religions'. For the first time, therefore, the basic curriculum of children and young people in our schools will not be meeting the legal standards unless 'they are taught the teaching' of the principal *non*-Christian religions in Great Britain.

The Act's religious provisions also 'imply a certain distance' from the obligation to 'teach' *Christianity*. Whatever syllabus was drawn up, it had only to 'reflect' and 'take account' of Christianity. It was clear to Hull therefore, that this left 'a wide margin of educational discretion' and that the Act would prove flexible enough 'to be adaptable to the needs of most situations in England and Wales'.[133]

Even though it came from someone whose Christian commitment and whose goodwill were beyond question, it was an announcement that anybody who wanted to could drive a coach and horses through the Act, and for the immediate good of non-Christian children (and perhaps also for the ultimate good of Christianity) he or she ought to do so.

In an editorial in the *British Journal of Religious Education* in the summer of 1989, Hull again turned his attention to the religious-worship provisions of the 1988 Act. In the normal run of acts of worship,[134] those 'wholly or mainly of a broadly Christian character', he argues, two out of three acts of worship a week need not mention Christianity at all. The one out of the three that did mention Christianity, he says, could deal with five verses from the Koran, as long as there were, say, six verses from the Psalms.

Care for the 'spirituality' of *all* the pupils in a school, Hull implies, is incompatible with acts of worship according to the tenets of any particular faith. 'Even when it has been found necessary as a last resort to seek a determination from SACRE for some acts of collective worship to be distinctive of a religious faith, we may still hope that the result will be a school which cares for and encourages the spirituality of all its pupils.'[135]

As a comment on Hull's contribution: all that was required to render the 1988 Act's Christian provisions nugatory was to create general uncertainty about their meaning and practical implications for the school. If that were achieved, syllabus conferences could continue to do what they had been doing since 1970. They could continue to produce syllabuses that dealt 'neutrally' with several religious faiths and magical and occult practices; with political doctrines, especially varieties of Marxism; and with atheistic views of human life.

Head teachers were given the explicit duty to carry out the Christian provisions of the 1988 Education Reform Act.[136] But in 1993 a report by the Religious Education Council disclosed that not only were most state schools failing to abide by the law of the land as laid down in the 1988 Act, *so were many Church of England schools*—and sometimes fudging their statistical returns to hide the fact.[137] At its annual conference in June 1994 the National Association of Head Teachers had before it a survey that showed that 70 per cent 'could not' hold a daily act of collective worship, and that 60 per cent 'could not' deliver the religious education curriculum. The general secretary of the association insisted that moral values could be taught outside the context of religious assemblies and RE lessons.[138]

The Ealing case

Four LEAs published new agreed syllabuses in 1989: Cornwall in March, Rotherham, Ealing and Oldham in June. Two were published in 1990: North Tyneside in May and Newcastle—in draft—in November. None of them demonstrated a major shift as a result of the new Act.

There was a local appeal against the London Borough of Ealing's agreed syllabus. During the appeal hearing an official of the London Diocesan Board for Schools admitted that there was no specifically Christian content in the syllabus, and that neither God, the Bible, nor Jesus Christ were mentioned in it. The next of the new London syllabuses was that for the Borough of Newham. It too was devoid of specifically Christian content.

Ealing's syllabus conference had discussed Section 8 (3) of the 1988 Act. It was argued on one side that it meant that the syllabus must be based on the Christian traditions, and must provide for teaching in other faiths where sufficient numbers of these faiths were represented in the classrooms. According to the Rev. Neil Richardson, the Anglican vicar who was chairman of the syllabus conference, this argument was immediately dismissed as 'divisive', and thus counter to the philosophy of inclusive education promoted within Ealing's schools.

The complaint against the Ealing syllabus was turned down by the Ealing local education authority and the complainant appealed to the secretary of state. The Department for Education (DFE) took legal advice, and counsel's opinion was that Ealing LEA had failed to comply with the 1988 Act. As a result of that legal opinion, the Department sent out a guidance letter saying that all syllabuses must give guidance on what 'traditions, learning, teaching and festivals were going to be *taught*' about *Christianity*.[139] 'Content-free' syllabuses did not comply with the law.

But when the National Curriculum Council reported on all the syllabuses adopted under the 1988 Act, it found that 'not a single syllabus matched all the legal requirements', and that only four out of the 27 studied 'went even part of the way'.[140] The Church of England had the right to veto illegal syllabuses. One of the main defects was that they lacked specific Christian content. Thirty senior members of the General Synod of the Church of England therefore wrote to *The Times* to criticise the Church of England authorities for their negligence.[141]

The National Curriculum Advisory Authorities

The Education Secretary, John Patten, asked the National Curriculum Council (NCC)—soon to be merged into a new School Curriculum and Assessment Authority (SCAA)—to define the content of religious education syllabuses. Six working groups were set up, one for Christianity and one for each of the five other principal faiths. When they had reported, the SCAA was then asked to produce national model syllabuses for the guidance of the local bodies responsible for producing the agreed syllabuses for their own areas. Mrs Barbara Wintersgill was appointed as curriculum officer for religious education, and in October 1993 a monitoring group was set up. The DFE issued new legal guidance on the 1988 Act. This prompted the non-Christian faith members of the monitoring group to send a letter to the chairman of SCAA on the model sylla-buses that the majority on the monitoring group had approved:

> At a time when fascism and religious persecution are on the increase and the British National Party has succeeded in a democratic election, pupils and teachers need clear guidance that although Britain is a nominally Christian country, citizens of all faiths or none are indeed equal under the law. In our view this is not the message being delivered by the model syllabuses as they currently stand.[142]

When the model syllabuses were ready to be distributed for consultation, four of the five non-Christian representatives of the monitoring group issued a press release criticising their Christian bias.[143] The guidance booklet from the DFE confirmed that Christianity should 'predominate' as a whole and at each key stage, constituting at least 50 per cent of the religious education syllabus in all schools. The syllabus as a whole must also 'represent all of the principal religions represented in this country'.[144]

The Education Acts of 1944 and 1988 laid upon education authorities the duty to promote the spiritual, moral, mental and physical education of pupils in their schools. Both listed spiritual first and moral second. The Qualifications and Curriculum Authority (QCA) stated that *its* mission was to promote education in the interests of individuals, the economy and society, in that order. This was a quite different 'mission' from the Education Acts. This list of priorities was highly acceptable, of course, to many people. There were many pressure groups whose agenda it was, for many different reasons, to promote the priority of the individual over the social, and of the economic over the spiritual. But these were not the priorities decided by Parliament.

'Religious studies' *as an examination subject* raises separate and different questions from the 'religious education' and 'worship' requirements of the Education Acts. But the content of the religious studies examinations cannot but influence the attitude of pupils generally to religious education and worship. The QCA subject criteria for A-level religious studies are rigorously secular.

The pupils' approach is to be, on the one hand, 'critical' and on the other 'empathetic', in that order.[145] Of course the secular study of religions (in the plural) in the manner of Ernst Troeltsch and Max Weber (for example) required empathy and the suspension of judgement. That did not imply promiscuous 'criticism'. It implied, once accumulated data on content and consequences permitted it, *responsible assessment* of comparative strengths and weaknesses when judged against seriously considered criteria of better and worse.[146]

These courses purport to aim at diversity and open-mindedness. What they *produce*, however, (and they could hardly do otherwise), is a uniform type of pupil with only one view of the world, self-centred, relativistic and either know-all or know-nothing, cynical or apathetic. Pupils choose whatever reaches their standards of acceptability, and reject whatever does not. It is up to them, in effect, to choose between 'Jesus bids us shine with a pure, clear light' and 'I get the party crackin' with the s*** that I be spittin'. So they switch on their computers and call in a rapper from the world-wide web—and, between a hymn and a rant, Eminem is far and away the pupils' popular choice.

Post-1970 religious education is a sort of Copernican revolution in reverse. The sun and the stars no longer revolve around the earth. But all that is supernatural now revolves around the opinion of the school child.[147]

3

Church of England
School Provision

In considering school provision, it is important to bear in mind that good education and high levels of school attendance, though normally closely related to each other, are not identical. Expensively-provided schools can fail in a culture hostile to self-improvement. Cultures valuing education highly can produce self-improvement with poor and few schools.

G.M. Trevelyan wrote that, at the end of the seventeenth century a fair proportion of the people, 'even in remote villages', were literate. 'It was an age of reading and writing in the conduct of the ordinary affairs of life.' But the 'uneducated' received their education, including politics, less from the school than from chapel and church.[1]

The high degree of English working-class literacy at the beginning of the nineteenth century is shown in the fact that religious tracts enjoyed such a large circulation. But literacy meant also a wide circulation for subversive political literature. Thomas Paine's shocking work, *The Rights of Man*, sold one and a half million copies. Samuel Bamford, the 'weaver poet', said that William Cobbett was 'read on nearly every cottage hearth in the manufacturing districts of South Lancashire'. Two hundred thousand copies of Cobbett's *Address to the Journeymen and Labourers* were sold in two months.

James Mill, writing in 1813, said that he could speak decidedly from his own observations and inquiries on the rapid progress that 'the *love* of education' was making among the lower orders in England. Even around London, far from the most virtuous part of the kingdom, he says, there was hardly a village without a school, and there were few children, boys or girls, who were not taught to read and write. In 1826 he wrote that reading, writing and 'accounts' were 'the requirements now common to the lowest of the people'.[2]

For the first third of the nineteenth century the state was anxious to *restrict* the uses of literacy, if not working-class literacy itself, by closing public reading rooms, withdrawing licences from public houses receiving newspapers, and by imposing swingeing duties and taxes on newspapers to put them out of reach of the working man. Advertising duties were not removed until 1853, stamp taxes until 1855 and excise taxes on paper until 1861.

In 1840, out of 843 coal miners employed in the collieries at Wallsend, West Towneley, Benwell, Elswick and Backworth, 665 could read, just short of 80 per cent. A survey of literacy in Hull in 1839 found that among 14,526 people aged 21 and over, 97 per cent of them had attended day or evening school, and 92 per cent of them could read.[3] In the younger generation, one study showed that even among the most 'deprived' and 'excluded', *pauper* children, 87 per cent could read to some extent.[4] (By contrast, more than a century later the literacy rate in Portugal—according to UNESCO—was 55-60 per cent, in Egypt 20-25 per cent, and in Algeria 15-20 per cent.)[5]

If it be said that terms such as 'reading ability' are too vague to be the basis of reliable figures, one justification for nevertheless treating them as being of some value is that there was 'remarkable consistency' between the figures from different investigators and types of survey in different parts of the country.[6] R.K. Webb suggests, furthermore, that many of the investigators were reformers, attacking the deficiencies of educational arrangements. They were therefore more likely to dwell on the unsavoury fact of illiteracy than exaggerate the reading abilities of working people. Webb's own estimate was that in the late 1830s between two-thirds and three-quarters of the working class was literate. Most of the 'respectable poor', as he calls them, 'the great political potential in English political life', were literate.[7]

That a bridegroom used his signature rather than made his mark on the wedding register is not a good indication of how literate he was. But the change in the proportion of bridegrooms using their signature is an index of the *rise* in literacy. In 1851 just under 70 per cent of bridegrooms used their signature. By 1861 the proportion had risen to 75 per cent. In 1871, the beginning of the Board school era, the percentage was 81 per cent. The addition of the Board schools to the Church of England and other voluntary schools maintained this rate of increase. The figure in 1881 was 86 per cent, in 1891 it was 94 per cent, and in 1900 it was 97 per cent. 'The Forster Act was responsible for the mopping up operation by which the *very poor children,* living in slums or in remote country regions, were taught to read.'[8] Raymond Williams, a prominent and highly re-spected left-wing intellectual in his time, wrote in 1961 that 'there was no sudden opening of the floodgates of literacy as a result of the 1870 Education Act'.[9] H.J. Perkins made the same point in *History Today*: it was untrue that the modern popular press grew in direct response to the literacy created by the Board schools, even though 'no historical myth dies harder'.

The Numerical Contribution of Church of England Schools to the School System in the Nineteenth and Twentieth Centuries

In 1818, a parliamentary select committee reported that there had been a marked increase in the proportion of children in schools from the beginning of the century. This surge was due, the committee said, not only to the work of the National Society and other such organisations, but also to the increased willingness and interest of parents to send their children to school, and to pay the fees that were nearly always asked.[10]

When the first state subsidy to education was approved in 1833, Parliament authorised another survey that showed that the number of children in school had nearly tripled, from 478,000 in 1818 to 1,294,000 in 1834.[11] Lord Brougham said of the increase that the machinery of education funded by parents out of their own earnings, supplemented by philanthropy to help those who could not afford it, was in 'steady, constant and rapid movement', and that the state could easily stop this momentum by trying to accelerate it.[12] The government, in giving an annual grant of £20,000 to cover all state aid for school building had, in West's words, 'jumped into the saddle of a horse that was already galloping'.[13]

The Census of 1851 provided details of the number of 'private' and 'public' schools that were established in each of the ten years 1841-50 (figures on schools closing each year were not supplied). 'Private' schools were those that derived their income solely from fee payments and whose objective was the pecuniary advantage of the proprietor. A school was a 'public' school if it was supported in any degree for aims other than pecuniary advantage. The figures for private and public schools established in the year 1841 were 688 and 415 respectively. The annual growth in private schools was more or less steady throughout the decade. Public school foundation lay within the range 372 in the year 1842 to 616 in the year 1850. According to the Census, by 1851 there were 17,000 Church of England schools. More than two million children were in day schools of all types.[14]

The Newcastle Commission 1859-61 calculated that, in 1858, 2,535,000 children were in day schools, either 'inspected' (state-subsidised) schools, including the Church of England schools, or 'non-inspected' (completely private) schools. Of these 2,535,000, 2,334,000 were children of the 'poorer classes'.

On the basis that children between the ages of three and 15 spent 5.7 years in elementary school, the Newcastle Commission calculated that 2,656,000 ought to have been in day school. The shortfall was on this calculation fewer than 121,000, 4.5 per cent of the child population. The 4.5 per cent who were not at day school was accounted for partly by infirmities and home tuition.

The commissioners concluded that there was no large district destitute of schools, nor any large section of the population sharply marked off from the rest as requiring some 'special and stringent system of treatment'.[15]

The Newcastle Commission's statistics had been produced by five commissioners and ten assistant commissioners over a period of three years, and covered the whole of England and Wales. The statistics that were used to justify the 1870 Act were collected by two Home Office inspectors over a period of a few months. They only covered Birmingham, Liverpool, Manchester and Leeds.

We may take the example of Liverpool to show how the statistics of the three Home Office inspectors were used to demonstrate a vast shortfall in school provision. In Liverpool there were 80,000 children aged five to 13. The inspectors reported—and Forster repeated—that 20,000 attended no school whatsoever, and another 20,000 attended schools that were entirely useless. *On that basis 40,000 out of 80,000 were receiving no school education at all, or as good as no school education.* This is the origin of the oft-repeated statement that at the time of the 1870 Act 'only half of the children in the country were educated at all'.[16]

So far as the figure of 20,000 'attending no school whatsoever' is concerned, however, this is a startling *non sequitur*. School attendance even to the age of *eleven* was not made compulsory until 1893. The Newcastle Commission had found that children were at school for about six years, not eight (from the age of five to the child's thirteenth birthday). On the basis of six years at school, and not eight, the Liverpool school population would have been 60,000—and that is how many children the Home Office inspectors in fact found.

The 20,000 'missing' children had not received 'no education', they had received the six years of education normal at the time. The six years of education was not much improved on by the Board schools. The raising of the school-leaving age to 14, then 15, then 16 had to wait for many years.[17]

Between 1870 and 1891 the providers of voluntary schools produced school accommodation for an additional 1.5 million pupils. There was also, however, considerable transfer of Church of England schools into the Board school sector—792 between 1870 and 1886, for example.[18]

Though the reality of duality between the state and voluntary components of school education was present in

the 1870 Act, the term 'dual system' is strictly applicable
only to the situation created by the Education Act of 1902.

In introducing the Bill that became the 1902 Act, A.J.
Balfour referred to the increasing difficulties being experienced by voluntary schools in reaching the rising standards
of the state schools. The fault was not, he said, a diminution
in philanthropy. Some of their opponents, Balfour said, put
down the growing difficulties of voluntary schools to the
want of liberality on the part of their subscribers. But it was
the rapid expansion of the voluntary schools during the
1870s that had placed on the Churches, he said, a burden
they found increasingly difficult to carry in the new circumstances of state regulation and the competition of the wholly
state-financed schools. They received *no* aid from the *rates*,
and they earned from the Education Department a slightly
smaller grant than the Board schools. But they were now
required by law to put their buildings into repair, to add
classrooms, and to provide, for example, cloakrooms to bring
the sanitation up to the standards of the time. They were
therefore compelled to economise by employing more
unqualified teachers, paying smaller salaries, and purchas-
ing less equipment than the Board schools. Though there
was no reason to think that subscribers were any less
numerous or generous than in the past, Balfour said, the
fact remained that:

> after all the great efforts of the voluntary subscriber and after all
> the aid given by the National Exchequer, the voluntary schools are
> in many cases not adequately equipped and not as well fitted as
> they should be to carry out the great part which they are inevitably
> destined to play in our system of national education.[19]

At the time of the 1902 Education Act there were 12,000
Church of England voluntary schools. Together with the
2,000 schools of other religious bodies, the voluntary schools
educated more than 3,000,000 pupils. The 5,700 Board
schools educated 2,600,000 pupils. Roman Catholic schools
accounted for five per cent of state and state-aided school
pupils.[20]

All the schools in the dual system were referred to as
'maintained' schools, since they were wholly or partly

maintained by public money. For some purposes the council schools (the former Board schools) were distinct, notably in the inspection of religious teaching. But for many purposes the maintained church schools and the maintained council schools were organised under the same local authorities.

In the period following the passing of the 1902 Act, the Church of England continued to lack the capital to match the quality of premises and equipment of the state schools. Even so, at the outbreak of the second world war all the church schools, including the Church of England schools, were providing education for one third of children of school age.

The Education Act 1944 distinguished between 'county' and 'voluntary' schools. County schools were those that had been either established by public money, or had at some stage been handed over by a voluntary body to the local education authority.

In 1950 there were 844,000 pupils in Church of England primary schools. This figure had fallen to 740,000 by 2000. By contrast, Roman Catholic primary school rolls had risen from 329,000 in 1950 to 411,000 in 2000.

In the Church of England secondary school sector there were 64,000 pupils in 1950. This figure had risen to 150,000 by 2000. But while there had been fewer Roman Catholic secondary school pupils in 1950 than Church of England secondary school pupils, by 2000 there were more than twice as many Roman Catholic as Church of England secondary school pupils, 309,000.[21]

4

The Civilisation Motive

The most influential Reader on educational sociology in the early 1960s, *Education, Economy and Society*, devoted one of its six sections to the social functions of schools, and changes in them over time.[1] At one theoretical extreme, schools can function only to foster the separate development of each individual child's unique 'personality' and its self-chosen goals. At the other theoretical extreme, schools can function only to fit the child to fulfil dutifully some role for the benefit of 'society'. In real life a society's schools lie somewhere between the two extremes: some societies have schools that are closer to the child-centred pole, some closer to the social-function pole.

David Glass says in *Education, Economy and Society* that the English elementary school until well into the twentieth century, whether provided by the Church of England or the state, gave priority to the social function, what he called the 'civilisation motive'.[2] One of the explicit purposes of nineteenth and (decreasingly) of twentieth century school education was, Glass remarks, to 'gentle the masses'.

The Nineteenth Century

The Royal Commission of 1858 said that 'a good set of schools civilises a whole neighbourhood'. The 'religious and moral influence' of the public elementary school was very great, 'greater than their intellectual influence'. And this, *'the most important* function of the schools', was 'the one they best perform'.[3]

Forster, in introducing the 1870 Education Bill, spoke of the school as a defence against crime and against other dangers to 'the community'. Speaking of the 1867 enfranchisement of urban working men he said, 'Now that we have

78

given them political power, we must not wait any longer to give them education'.[4] We must educate our masters to be capable of being good citizens.

Marx's friend Engels is full of frustrated admiration for the success of this 'civilising' or, pejoratively, 'gentling' component of English school education. He was particularly frustrated by the success of the contribution of religious education to it.

Writing in 1892, he contrasted the law-abiding English working man with the revolutionary proletarian of France and Germany in terms that might well surprise people who look to Marxism to justify their belief that religion is powerless and material conditions paramount.

The British capitalist had spent thousands and tens of thousands in self-imposed taxes, year after year, upon the evangelisation of the lower orders. He had done it through the schools, most recently by imposing rates upon himself and (Engels said) ensuring that parsons formed the majority on the new School Boards.

He had done it through 'his own native religious machinery'. He had not been above importing American evangelists like Moody and Sankey, 'the greatest organisers in existence of religion as a trade'. He had even accepted the dangerous aid of the Salvation Army, 'which revives the propaganda of early Christianity, appeals to the poor ... and thus fosters an element of early Christian class antagonism'.

The French and German capitalists, Engels continued, were now silently dropping their disastrous free thought. One by one they were 'turning pious in their outward behaviour, spoke well of the Church, its dogmas and rites, and even conformed to the latter as far as could not be helped'. In doing so, they were imitating what the British capitalist had been doing for 50 years, 'regardless of the sneers of his Continental compeers'. The sophisticated continentals had come to grief with their materialism. *'Die Religion muß dem Volk erhalten werden*—religion must be kept alive for the people. Now, if ever, the people must be kept in order by moral means, and *the first and foremost of all moral means of action upon the masses is and*

remains—religion.' The French and Germans had belatedly
realised that this was the only and last means, Engels said,
to save their societies from utter ruin from the socialists
and revolutionaries. 'Unfortunately for themselves, they did
not find this out until they had done their best to break up
religion for ever.'

The practical result was that at any rate until the late
1870s[5] 'the British workman ... was the model workman,
whose respectful regard for the position of his master, and
whose self-restraining modesty in claiming rights for
himself, consoled our German economists of the *Katheder*-
socialist school for the incurable communistic and revolutionary tendencies of their own working men at home'.

'British respectability' had signally triumphed, Engels
wrote, over 'the free thought and religious laxity of the
Continental bourgeoisie'. The English middle class—good
men of business as they were—had seen farther than the
German professors. 'Now it was the turn of the British
bourgeois to sneer and say, "Why, you fools, I could have
told you that two hundred years ago!"'[6]

The First Half of the Twentieth Century

In 1925 Trotsky found that the English working classes
were still hopelessly religious, respectable and proud of
their 'pigsty' of parliamentary democracy.[7]

From the opposite end of the spectrum, a pamphlet on
Christian citizenship produced at about the same time
could make the casual remark that such things as theft and
drunkenness were no long serious problems in an England
that had seen the 'benefits of generations of advancing
Christian civilisation'—an observation that the statistics on
crime and alcohol consumption in 1920s' England fully
supported.[8]

Four years later the noted educationalist Sir Cyril
Norwood celebrated the same things as Engels and Trotsky
had regretted. Norwood argued that the elementary school
was the main instrument in preventing 'theories of revolt
and destruction' obtaining any real hold upon the people of
this country.[9]

Lowndes's *The Silent Social Revolution*, published in 1937, was a familiar university text book until at least the early 1950s. The English, he wrote, 'have probably for centuries been as decent, as commonsensical and as slow to anger as any people'. But if anyone doubted the refinement of these qualities that the schools had achieved, he wrote, let him ask what would have happened in the mid-1930s in the event of a sudden cessation of civil authority in some town he knew—and then ask himself what would have happened 40 years before. Perhaps he could actually recall such occasions. If not, he said, let the doubter read contemporary descriptions of the scenes in London during the 'Sack of the West End' in 1884, or on 'Bloody Sunday', in 1887.

Then let him pass forward to the 'Black Sunday' riots in Liverpool during 1911, when the German war lords, perhaps *miscalculating the resources of civilisation which we had already accumulated* and thinking a revolution on the continental model was imminent, are said to have sent the German fleet into the North Sea prepared for an attack on an England fatally weakened by civil strife.

Let him follow this up by reading the far less serious, because far less bitter, scenes which accompanied the withdrawal of services by the local police ten years later in the same town.

Finally, let him reflect on the almost complete absence of any serious civil disorder, either in Liverpool or elsewhere, during the general stoppage of 1926.

The contribution that the school system had made to the 'cleanliness, orderliness, sobriety and self-respect', Lowndes wrote, 'must always, perhaps, seem to *outweigh all other gains*'.[10]

A visitor to any English elementary school in the mid-1930s, he wrote, would observe the 'the economy and efficiency of the discipline. He would note its atmosphere of orderliness and precision', and would carry away 'an indelible impression' of 'good manners and politeness'. Lest these things should be taken for granted in 1935, Lowndes said, it would be well to remind the visitor that, barely 50 years before, 'the attendance officer who wished to pene-

trate one of these slums from which some of the children
still come had to take *a police officer* with him'.[11]

The Second Half of the Twentieth Century

Child-centred education had been an important, benign and
growing component in school philosophy and practice for
many decades before the 1960s. The 1960s saw it achieve
sudden overweening dominance. Highly permissive educational ideas were generated and applauded in this country,
and imported along with the more exciting ideas of the
revolutionary student movements in Germany and France.

The spirit of the 1960s and 1970s can be recaptured
slightly even today. In February 2001 *Libération* recalled
that as a *soixante-huitard* ('nineteen-sixty-eighter') the
French Minister of Education, Jack Lang, had signed a
petition criticising a prison sentence meted out to three
paedophiles. The petition was followed by an open letter
from a group of sixty-eighter intellectuals demanding a
'recognition of the right of children ... to conduct relationships with whomsoever they want'.

Daniel Cohn-Bendit, 'Danny the Red', one of the leaders
of the student radicals in the 1960s and 1970s, published an
article in 1975 that gave an explicit and vivid account of his
sexual interaction with children in the kindergarten where
he had been a teacher. In reality, he said in 2001, he
believed that paedophilia was 'one the most despicable
crimes that could exist'. He had written falsehoods in 1975,
he says, as a matter of 'pure provocation'. They were the
result of his 'indefensible thoughtlessness' in attempting to
'shock the bourgeoisie'.[12] That he had thought this was an
appropriate way in which to do so, however, reveals the
strength of the doctrine of the time that 'it is only forbidden
to forbid'.

In England by the year 2001, at the end of a period of
state-supported education that began in 1833, with an
annual grant that amounted in total for all schools in the
country to £20,000, a newspaper headline announced that
teachers in England were be to be taught self-defence as
part of a £22 million package to improve the security of

schools and their staffs. Estelle Morris, the school standards minister, said the money would be spent also on surveillance cameras, secure door-entry systems and strengthening the perimeter walls of schools. This public money brought to £88 million the total spent on school security alone since the murder of a headmaster, Philip Lawrence, outside his west London comprehensive school in December 1995. The report called the £88 million spent over six years, in trying to cope with violence and destruction in the schools, public 'investment'.[13]

5

The Culture Wars 1950-2001

A history of Church of England school education must pay some attention to the layered contexts in which that history has been played out. If we consider only the past 50 years, society has greatly changed. School practice has changed. State education has grown in influence. The religious and moral assumptions of politicians who decide what money Church of England schools will receive, and on what conditions, have changed. The theological propositions and ethical standards that the hierarchy of the Church of England takes seriously have changed. Church of England schools operate within the general culture of their time. In the past 50 years the general culture has shifted sharply away not only from support for the Church of England but from support for any religion, and not only from any particular version of inculcated and sanctioned morality, but from 'moralising' at all.

Since the 1950s, the tempo of secularisation has been stepped up. Society has become steadily more materialistic, egoistic and hedonistic. In this country, materialism has been a success in its own terms. Civil society has in various ways deteriorated. There is far more crime than 50 years ago, worse riots have erupted far more frequently, and 'enlightened' activists much more commonly use lethal terror in the pursuit of their 'justice'. But there has been no major international war for us; nor in England has there been, 'deep as hell itself, the avenging draught of civil slaughter'.[1] There is squalor and vandalism in the streets. But there are goods of endless variety and secure supply in the palatial and orderly supermarkets and shopping malls. The family of life-long monogamy as a firmly preferred institution has been destroyed. But, physically, the average dwelling and its amenities has improved out of all recognition. Publicly sanctioned customs and attitudes that held the number of disasters or problems in private life at a low level—moral protection—have been weakened. But physical and chemical remedies, subsidised or paid for entirely by the state, have been made widely and easily available. In the circumstances of rising economic prosperity for most people, egoistic liberty and self-regarding hedonistic lifestyles are generally experienced by adults as benefits.

Church of England schools, more and more heavily subsided by the state, have had to adjust to the fashionable philosophies dominant from time to time in the state education system, and the state education system has been heavily influenced by the constant movement of the general culture away from anything smacking of 'indoctrination' or the authoritative presentation of facts or values. In devising religious education suitable for the wholly state school, the Church of England has come to apply state-school religious education to its own pupils. Church of England archbishops, bishops and other clergy have sought with varying degrees of enthusiasm and success to come to terms with modernity.[2]

People used to say, 'If you sup with the devil, use a long spoon'. The title of this chapter could have been, 'Too short a spoon'.

During the violent student disturbances of the 1960s and 1970s one graffito became famous. It was one of William Blake's 'Proverbs of Hell'. 'The tigers of wrath are wiser than the horses of instruction.' Blake's 'Proverbs of *Hell*' were quoted as if they were insightful advice on how a wise person will lead his or her life. 'The lust of the goat is the bounty of God'; 'The road of excess leads to the palace of wisdom'; 'If a fool would persist in his folly he would become wise', and so forth.[3]

Advocating a life of self-regarding 'wrath', 'lust' and 'excess' was not, traditionally, a Church of England thing to do, permit or recommend. Blake in his proverbs of Heaven and Hell was presenting a 'conflict of visions', to use Thomas Sowell's phrase.[4]

Ways of Looking at the World and Behaving in It

The study of the different 'definitions of the situation' held by different groups and persons was an important strand in sociology in the twentieth century. Different visions of the world and eternity, and the associated emotional and practical responses to them, were the essence of what university sociologists studied when the influence of academic sociology was at its height in the 1950s and for much of the 1960s.

These were not necessarily conflicting visions and emotions, still less irreconcilable ones. Societies and organisations essentially work by drawing together in co-operation sets of people with different functions based on their different conceptual schemes of what the world and the spirit are like, and how they ought to act in relation to them. Such coherent or harmonious differences are described by Paul when he speaks of diversities of gifts, administrations and operations that are unified by the same Spirit.[5]

In innumerable variations different sets of people can be categorised according to what *they think* is factually true about human nature; about the physical world of resources and scarcity; and about the spiritual realm.

Different sets of people then have different beliefs about the best way, morally or practically, to respond to what they think is true.

The purely empirical question of what a given set of people *regard as* 'fact' is separate, that is, from the equally empirical question of what they *regard as* 'moral' or expedient. People can form a single category in respect of their shared beliefs about what the 'facts' are (whether they are right about the facts or not). They can nevertheless form distinctly different groups on the basis of what they should do in the light of the 'facts' as they believe them to be, and how they respond emotionally to them.

Irreconcilable Visions of Man and Morals

This kind of sociology sought to 'understand' (potentially) all or any variations of group perceptions of fact and value.

Not all group perceptions of fact and value clash with one another, however bizarre one or more of the perceptions might be.

But there *are* irreconcilable world-views. Simplified dichotomous accounts of people's fundamentally opposing views of what the facts are, what good behaviour is, and by what criteria people should properly decide what is true and good are common throughout written history.

The sacred versus *the profane*

One of the founders of sociology as a university subject, Emile Durkheim, believed that the distinction made *or neglected* between the sacred and profane, the untouchable and the mundane, was basic to the understanding of the conduct of any society or group within it. What do people approach as matters of everyday practical life, to be used or discarded as expediency dictates? What do people approach in the most drastically different spirit possible, with awe and reverence, as phenomena forever outside their puny competence, and as injunctions that they have no right to question, much less defy?[6]

The realm of the sacred or holy is not properly seen as that of the unquestionably moral, for what is merely moral remains within the province of human manipulation. The sacred, the holy, is the province of 'the completely other, the ineffable, supernatural, transcendental'. It is not to be interfered with by mere human beings at all, for whatever 'good' reason they might think they have.[7]

There is a story about 'the sacred' in 1 Chronicles 13: 9-11. Uzza did not have the necessary sanctity for touching the ark of the covenant. One of the oxen carrying it stumbled. The unqualified Uzza put out his hand to hold it. 'And the anger of the Lord was kindled against Uzza, and he smote him ... and he died before God.' Even David thought that God had been utterly unreasonable, and was 'displeased' —but as a result of the episode he was 'afraid before God that day'.

In 1848, Marx and Engels, in one of their most forceful statements, described the replacement of the sacred by the profane in capitalist societies.

> All fixed, fast-frozen relations, with their train of ancient and
> honoured prejudices and opinions, are swept away, all new-formed
> ones become antiquated before they can ossify. All that is solid
> melts into air, all that is holy is profaned, and every man is at last
> compelled to face with sober senses the real conditions of life, and
> his relations with his kind.[8]

This passage remains a vivid description of desacral-
isation, even though Engels later admitted that he and
Marx had been premature in describing England in those
terms. As far as England was concerned, he acknowledged
half-a-century later, there had been a great reinstatement
of the sacred through Victorian religiosity.[9]

But the context within which Church of England school
education has worked for the past 50 years has been one
which *has* seen a marked acceleration in the decline in
'sacred' things. Medicine and politics have brought more
and more of these formerly 'holy' areas of human life and
the treatment of the dead within the sphere of everyday
routine.

Modern art, drama and popular entertainment have been
preoccupied with seeking out what is 'sacred' precisely *in
order* to profane it. The disappearance of the sacred is not
a problem only for the Church of England and its schools.
For from the opposite standpoint, both art and entertainment, confronted with the thoroughly blasé audiences they
have created, face the problem (apparently unbeknown to
them) that they have almost exhausted their own raw
material. The century-long project of 'shocking the bourgeoisie' itself loses all its meaning when there are so few
English people left, bourgeois or respectable working class,
whose sense of the sacred make them shockable by any
profanity at all.

Religious views versus *magical views of the world and of supernatural forces*

People act on the basis of their beliefs about the world and
supernatural forces. There is a radical difference between
those who believe that there are supernatural forces, as
compared with those who do not. But among those who do

believe in the supernatural, 'religion' and 'magic' are concepts based upon radically different ways in which they behave in relation to what they believe to be true. The vital distinction is familiar through Sir James Frazer's discussion of the point in *The Golden Bough*.[10] Magic is a matter of coercion, religion of supplication.[11]

The religious state of mind is preponderantly one of submission and reverence. The religious person acknowledges the superiority of the supernatural powers upon whose action his or her well-being depends. The religious person's behaviour is manifest in prayers, offerings and self-sacrifice.

Subordination, helplessness and so forth are feelings and attitudes that have diminished over the past 50 years, as part of the same process that has eroded the province of the sacred.

The believer in magical supernatural forces conceives them as being under the control of the qualified practitioner. The magician has earthly power over supernatural power. He or she works with a kind of arrogance, or at least self-assurance. If he or she uses the tested formula perfectly then, barring outside interference, the supernatural power has no choice but to obey.

People can believe in magic because sometimes it 'works'. It works by coincidence—if sufficient time is allowed, the desired event might well come about. (Just as astrology works for someone, if the forecast covers enough people.) It also sometimes works by psychological suggestion. Sickness curses work by somatic compliance. Doctors know well the importance of the psychological state of the patient in crucial illness or injury. Death curses work by 'thanatomania' (the suppression of the will to live). The records of anthropologists abound with such cases of successful magic.[12]

Generally, humility is now thought to be disgraceful. The *confidence* of the magician, which resembles the well-based confidence of the scientist, is more in keeping with the contemporary emphasis on self-esteem, control over one's own life, and mastery of the environment (whether to preserve or to exploit it). As G.K. Chesterton observed, when all-conquering man ceases to believe in God, he doesn't believe in nothing, he believes in anything.

Dionysus versus *Apollo*

Nietzsche discusses two other drastically different ways of perceiving and acting. Though he used religious names to label them, he applied them also to a wholly secular world where, as he had Zarathustra say, 'God is dead'.[13]

One he called Dionysian. The votary of Dionysus seeks the annihilation of the ordinary bonds and limits of existence. He or she values 'drunkenness', in the sense not restricted to the effects of alcohol. Some Dionysians induce their desired state of intoxication by mortification of the flesh, crowd hysteria, sexual ecstasy however achieved, or by imbibing what Bernard Bosanquet somewhere called 'the dangerous drug of violence'. Others, as isolated individuals or as participants, do so with chemical substances such as alcohol, cannabis, or opium—in many societies with cultural or sect approval. Dionysians actively seek hallucinations and frenzy. In the original Dionysian cults which placed the highest value on intoxicated, orgiastic and orgasmic sex, maenads (*mainomai* = rave) played a prominent part, and sometimes a part that with extreme savagery excluded men.

The other way of thinking and acting Nietzsche called Apollonian. The Apollonian distrusts all this. He knows but one overriding law: '*measure* in the Hellenic sense'.[14] He keeps to the middle of the known road. He sticks to the map he was given. He does not meddle with disruptive psychological states; he abhors them. Even in the exaltation of the dance he 'remains what he is, and retains his civic name' —seemly, decorous, and 'decent'.[15]

In his *English Social History* G.M. Trevelyan provides a vivid insight into the mind of the cultivated Englishman in 1942, which he believed was the mind shared with most English people at that time. Writing of the early years of the reign of Charles II, he says:

> England was sound enough. But her courtiers and politicians were rotten. For the King himself and the younger generation of the

aristocracy had been demoralised by the break-up of their education and family life ... For these reasons a hard disbelief in virtue of any kind was characteristic of the restored leaders of politics and fashion, and was reflected in the early Restoration drama which depended on their patronage. One of the most successful pieces was Wycherley's *Country Wife*; the hero, by pretending to be a eunuch, secures admission to privacies which enable him to seduce women; one is expected to admire his character and proceedings. *In no other age, before or after, would such a plot-motive have appealed to any English audience.*[16]

In the past 50 years British society has moved distinctly along the continuum from the Apollonian towards the Dionysian pole. In the field of popular entertainment the shift has been remarkable. As Andrew Fletcher wisely observed, 'if a man were permitted to make all the ballads, he need not care who should make the laws', for he, not the legislator, would be the master of the nation's way of life.[17] We could say today, 'the pop songs, the soap operas, the films and the videos'.

In January 2001 a Mr Griffin, the owner of a sex-shop, was fined £5,826 after pleading guilty before York magistrates to the charge brought by the local authority that he had sold videos in his Grimsby and York shops that were only 'soft pornography', or were not reasonably pornographic at all (e.g. *Secrets of a Sensual Nurse* and *Confessions of a Sex Maniac*). His customers had thought from the titles they had selected for themselves that they were buying 'hard pornography'. Colin Romford, head of the trading standards department of the city of York, said, 'We responded to complaints from the public, both men and women ... They did not know exactly what they had bought until they had settled down to watch the films. In many cases they must have got a shock, hence the complaints'. Mr Griffen, apparently somewhat more old-fashioned than Mr Romford, said, 'I am amazed that people have the audacity to complain about things like that'.[18]

Victoria Harrington's study of the drinking habits of 1,790 young people in England and Wales found that 38 per cent of the 13-14-year-old boys and 35 per cent of the girls had been 'very drunk' at least once in the previous year.

Among the 15-16-year-old boys, 68 per cent and 57 per cent of the girls had been 'very drunk'. Among the 17-18 year olds the figures for being 'very drunk' were 80 per cent of the boys, and 75 per cent of the girls.[19]

The World Health Organisation's study of underage drinking in 29 countries found that it was almost non-existent in most of them, but that it was now high and increasing in England and Wales. In England a quarter of 13-year-old boys said that they had been drunk at least twice in their lives. Fourteen per cent of 11-year-old boys in England, and nine per cent of 11-year-old girls, reported that they drank alcohol at least once a week.[20]

The 'unconstrained' vision versus the 'constrained' vision

Thomas Sowell's pair of contrasting ways of looking at the mundane and spiritual world is the 'unconstrained vision' and the 'constrained vision'.

The moralistic unconstrained vision

Sowell's 'unconstrained vision' is not in its origin a Dionysian vision, though over time it has developed into one. To typify the unconstrained vision he takes what is today a thoroughly antiquated world-view, Godwin's *Enquiry Concerning Political Justice*.[21]

According to Godwin, following the *philosophes* of the French Enlightenment and being followed by a succession of 'progressive' politicians, educationalists and theologians, human beings are not self-centred by nature. They are directly capable of feeling other people's needs as even more important than their own. Selfishness was *caused by* the fear of punishment, and by the hope of reward. Practically, both were 'inimical to the improvement of the mind'. Morally, both were 'wrong in principle'. People in their natural state are capable of drawing the moral conclusion of self-sacrifice, and acting upon it. 'If a thousand men are to be benefited ... I am only an atom in comparison.' Existing men and women, existing children are selfish only because they have been *corrupted* by social training, social customs, and social control. The natural man, the natural child, is virtuous. All he needs is encouragement and freedom: his virtue and virtues will flower naturally.[22]

The Godwinian vision of man and society strongly characterised the Labour party from its inception until, say, the publication of Crosland's *Future of Socialism* in 1956 and Roy Jenkins' liberalising measures as Home Secretary in the Wilson government of 1964.[23]

Whatever their other differences, until the middle of the twentieth century the leaders of the Fabians, the Independent Labour Party (ILP), the Labour party and the trade unions, espoused a doctrine of virtuous, abstemious service to the community. (Some of them were in their private lives bohemians, and a few even libertines. Nearly all of these were renegades from the middle- and upper-middle-classes. But they had to be firmly closet bohemians.) In a predominantly protestant England, the rank and file were strongly (though not solely) recruited from the family-oriented, self-improving, intensely sober and respectable circles of the protestant chapels. Their vision was of the best of working-class culture, elevated, with its physical hardships removed.

> These things shall be! A loftier race
> Than e'er the world has known shall rise
> With flame of freedom in their souls
> And light of science in their eyes.
> New arts shall bloom of loftier mould,
> And mightier music thrill the skies,
> And every life shall be a song,
> When all the earth is paradise.[24]

The nationalisation of the health service, the schools, and social security, were all based the upon the conception of reality and ethics—it could not have been based on any other—of an English working class that sought a standard of living no higher than that necessary for a productive life of work, wholesome, improving leisure and service to the community.

In this world-view, working-class life suffered less from the corruption of 'real' human nature than did the middle class, and certainly less than the aristocracy. Few people in their natural development would want to abuse a fair system. Those who were still contaminated for a time by the old habits of feudalism and capitalism, by their greed, selfishness or idleness, would be heartily condemned by their peers, and soon see the error of their ways.

The moralistic constrained vision

The 'constrained vision', by contrast, is that of those who believe that it is a fact of human nature, and therefore of religious, political, sexual, parental and neighbourhood life, that people are inevitably self-centred—and something moral must be done about that fact if society in any of its aspects is to function.

Adam Smith strongly affirms that human beings are by nature concerned with the welfare of other people, they suffer when other people suffer, and are joyful when other people are happy.[25] Religion, philosophy and common sense all point to the sense of duty, he says, not as the sole, but as properly and practically 'the ruling and governing' basis of conduct.[26] He talks about the genuine and deep distress of a benevolent and sensitive person in Europe to news of a disastrous earthquake in China. But, he says, when all his sincere and deeply felt humane sentiments over the ruin of a hundred million of his brethren had been once fairly expressed ... he would go to bed and 'snore with the most profound security'. Let the same benevolent man know that for some reason tomorrow he will certainly lose his little finger, 'and he will not sleep tonight'. With the exception of a few saints, his reaction is everybody's reaction.

Egocentricity *in the sense of this disproportion* is a basic constraint within which all teachers, parents, clergymen and politicians at all times and in all places have to work.[27] A person holding such a vision will emphasise the need for moralistic education and social control, and rate prudence highly, no less as a personal virtue than as a sound rule governing all aspects of community life.

In theological terms, of course, the unconstrained vision is close to that of the British-born heretic Pelagius, who was denounced by St Augustine of Hippo for his insistence on man's basically good moral nature and natural ability to choose the right path of conduct.[28] The constrained vision is

close to that of the Roman Catholic church and of the 1950s'
Church of England.

Institutionalised views of the world versus *private views of
the world*

As a result of their factual perceptions and moral evaluations about human nature, religion, the state, and non-state
social organisations, people distribute themselves along a
theoretical continuum from, at one extreme, those preferring a totalitarian *Gleichschaltung* (complete sameness of
fanatical beliefs) to those, at the other, who prefer a completely uncontrolled universal diversity, with as many
opinions as there are people—which easily ends up as the
complete sameness of no beliefs.

*The belief in the benefits of strong group views strongly
defended*

In the eighteenth century Edmund Burke had expressed in
his phrase 'the little platoons' the idea that freedom for
everyone was protected by the existence of many strong
groups each strongly protecting their own group views. In
the late eighteenth and in the nineteenth century a similar
suggestion had been made, notably by Alexis de Tocqueville.
He argued that, because strong intermediate groups had
been destroyed and not replaced, the French had moved
more than once towards unconstrained liberty, only to find
that they were again within the portals of authoritarian-
ism.[29] In the late nineteenth century Emile Durkheim
expressed the idea in terms of functional groups protecting
society against both the opposite evils of the stifling power
of the state and the chaos of *anomie*.[30]

The trauma of twentieth-century experiences with social
disorganisation followed by dictatorship suggested to many
notable writers that the continuum, from totalitarianism at
one pole to self-centred individualism unrooted in shared
communities of belief at the other, formed a loop, placing
the two extremes, after all, close to one another.[31]

Immediately after the second world war, Hannah Arendt
highlighted the role played in the emergence of the phen-
omenon of the totalitarian society by the decay or destruc-

tion of independent groups, from the host of permanently constituted small families, to large-scale institutions like the churches. 'Every group of people who begin to show signs of ... solidarity', she wrote, 'must be broken up ... for the sake of an atomised society that alone can be totally dominated.'[32]

In the past 50 years—and for long before—this problem has not presented itself in this country in any such extreme form. This is one of the features of what Germany's Foreign Minister, Joscha Fischer, called England's 'fortunate history'.[33] But it has appeared in this country in the form of the conflict between those who believe in the strong group representation of definite and diverse opinions, and those who believe in the equal validity of all opinions bearing on religion and morals—and even scientific data.

Sociology, before it was transformed by the radical movements of the late 1960s and 1970s, conceptualised this intermediate form as the conflict between the 'mass' society of unorganised individuals on the one hand, and on the other hand the 'pluralistic' society that contains many strong groups within it.

Strong-group, or institutional, pluralism was regarded by the early American sociologists as the form that all societies were taking in the modern world. C.H. Cooley wrote that modern conditions 'enlarge indefinitely the competition of ideas, and whatever has owed its persistence merely to lack of competition is likely to go, for that which is really *congenial to the choosing mind* will be all the more *cherished and increased*'.[34]

American sociologists of the same generation as S.M. Lipset, Reinhard Bendix, C. Wright Mills, David Riesman, R.A. Dahl, and Daniel Bell were preoccupied with the causes and consequences of the 'massification' of the liberal democracies.[35] Raymond Aron supported them in France, against the prevailing fashions of existentialism and communism; and, soon, against the assorted New Left theories of the generation of students who would demonstrate their enthusiasm, with guns in Germany, with paving stones in France and with tee-shirts in England, for Mao's China and Che Guevara's Cuba.[36]

The pluralistic society of groups, C. Wright Mills wrote, was based on the great hope that truth and justice would be carved out of society in the course of free discussion. People are presented with problems. They discuss them. They decide on them. Each person formulates his or her own viewpoint. Viewpoints are *organised, and they compete*. One viewpoint gains a majority for the time being. The current view of truth and justice then has consequences in private life and public policy, and these consequences are scrutinised and commented upon freely by strong groups in the public domain.[37] In his opinion, to grasp that we were moving from being a pluralistic society of strong groups into being a 'mass society' of amorphous indifference was to hold a key to the meaning of modern life.

According to these empirical researchers and theorists, people with similar world-views, strongly organised in groups and *open to persuasion by other groups*, were, in their effects, the protectors of both freedom and tolerance. The theory in its modern, research-based, sociological guise was formulated by Lipset, Martin and Trow in these words:

> Democratic rights have developed in societies largely through the struggles of various *groups*—class, religious, sectional, economic, professional—against one another and against the group that controls the state. Each interest group may *want* to carry its own will, but if no one group is strong enough to obtain complete power, the result is the development of tolerance. In large measure the development of the concept of tolerance, the recognition of the rights of groups with whom one disagrees *to compete* ... arose out of conflict among *strong and indestructible groups*.[38]

The individual in this system is exhorted to

Dare to be a Daniel!
Dare to stand alone!
Dare to have a purpose true!
Dare to make it known!

But he or she is also exhorted to unite with like-minded people, in solidarity and loyalty, to maintain, develop and foster the group's aims and methods, *while not merely permitting, but encouraging other people and groups to do the same.*

The most important three senses in which the full set of voluntary groups are 'voluntary' are, first, that no one is compelled to join, and every one is free to leave any group without any penalty but the loss of the privileges of membership. All individuals, members and non-members, therefore possess a very strong voting right in relation to every group for which they qualify—the right to vote with their feet.

Secondly, whatever individuals can do legally, the members can make into a general rule for membership. To the extent that private persons can legally do so, they can choose to associate with whomsoever they want on whatsoever conditions they wish. The organisation is not forced to admit dissidents from its purposes and procedures, nor is it forced to retain them.

Thirdly, no one who feels that some interest of his or hers is not represented is prevented from founding—or from attempting to found—a functioning voluntary association for purposes, and using means, that are legal for private persons. Everyone is free to undertake *what is for anyone* the extremely difficult and hazardous task of setting up a religious, social, economic or political organisation of people with like minds or interlocking interests.

The success and stability of such a system is based on (i) the self-discipline of the citizens and (ii) the predominant influence that appropriate manners and beliefs, not coercion, exert on the conduct of individuals.[39]

Everybody's opinion is equally worth considering, certainly without regard to his or her status, profession or wealth. But everybody's opinion is not equally worthy of being accepted. People *earn* the intellectual right to have their opinion preferred to that of others, from their relevant experience, from their intuitive wisdom, or by their having worked hard to unearth the best available data and having reflected seriously on the moral implications of them.[40]

Francis Fukuyama argued in three books well-received in the 1990s that appropriate legal structures and organisational institutions are critical to the success of modern societies. *But they are not by themselves sufficient to bring about success.* 'Liberal democracy has always depended on *certain cultural values* to work properly.' Many of the countries of Latin America, he argues, adopted formal political arrangements, formal legal systems and formal economic institutions patterned on the United States. But time and again they failed to make them work. Fukuyama says that this was because their *culture* was that of 'imperial and Latin Catholic traditions of Spain and Portugal', which hindered the growth of 'an independent civil society'.

By contrast, he writes, the United States had its origin in a distinctly different *culture*, that of 'sectarian Protestantism' and specifically British law and British public and private morality. There was therefore a tendency for American society to be self-organising in 'a myriad of voluntary associations and communities'. The vitality of this *culture* of a pluralistic civil society, Fukuyama says, 'was crucial for both the stability of its democratic institutions and its vibrant economy'.[41]

Tocqueville also attributes the American system of strong-group pluralism—among the Europeans of the North East and the Western USA—to what was specific about *British culture*. 'The English who emigrated three hundred years ago to found a democratic commonwealth on the shores of the New World had all learned to take part in public affairs in their mother country; they were conversant with trial by jury; they were accustomed to freedom of speech and of the press, to personal freedom, to the notion of rights *and the practice of them*. They carried to America their free *institutions* and manly *customs*.'[42] Neither the American Fukuyama nor the Frenchman Tocqueville can be accused of British chauvinism, nor was either of them referring to *race* at all.

The purpose of the school in a pluralistic society in this sense was to prepare children for making a choice between *profoundly important* alternatives, participation in strong groups, and competition between them. The school did this by equipping children with a moral compass and basic knowledge, the motivation to acquire more, and a sense of responsibility for playing a serious part in the ebb and flow of moral and factual discussions that affect private and public life. The result of doing otherwise is to produce what

A.E. Bestor called 'educational wastelands'. 'If schools are doing their job', he wrote,

> we should expect educators to point to the significant and indisput-able achievement in *raising the intellectual level of the nation* —measured perhaps by larger per capita circulation of *serious* books and magazines, by *definitely improving taste* in movies and radio programmes, by *higher* standards of political debate, by increased respect for freedom of speech and of thought.[43]

St Augustine of Hippo preceded John Stuart Mill in maintaining that truth is actually harmed more by the feeble indifference of its enemies rather than by their own and their enemies' robust mistakes. Those blinded by error train the church in wisdom, just as those depraved by wickedness train her in benevolence.[44]

In the mid-1960s the Roman Catholic church produced a powerful statement of the benefits to the whole of society of the system of strong group views strongly defended. In the view of *Gravissimum educationis*, the existence of strong groups with strong views was so important, that *for that reason* the education of their members' children should be assisted with state grants. It was the duty of every state, Pope Paul VI declared in that document, to see to it 'that public subsidies were paid out in such a way that parents were truly free to choose according to their conscience the schools they wanted for their children'.

The best kind of contemporary society is 'pluralistic' in the strong-group sense of pluralistic. Therefore the Roman Catholic church, *Gravissimum educationis* says, 'esteems highly' those civil authorities that honour religious freedom by providing public funds to cater for the *diverse* moral and religious principles through their schools. In those states that do so, the Catholic school was a means of 'fostering the *dialogue* between the Church and mankind, to the benefit of both'.[45] By implication, other such strong-group, state-aided schools would be making, in turn, their distinct and beneficial contributions to that vigorous dialogue.

The belief in weak opinions that everybody shares

'Pluralism' in the old sense of the word, then, described a functioning liberal democracy that drew its vigour from the participation of the ordinary citizen, as he or she acted through groups organised to further his or her causes or promote his or her beliefs. Participants were culturally conditioned to feel personal responsibility for the integrity of the institutional system, for compliance with the written and unwritten 'rules of the game'—the word and the spirit. The term was used to distinguish an effective liberal democracy from totalitarian or authoritarian systems. But it was also used to distinguish effective liberal democracies from mass societies where individuals were certainly 'free', but were left to their own devices to make moral and factual sense of the world. As isolated individuals they were naked before such blasts of organised commercial, political or social opinion as *were* directed at them.

Several perfectly serviceable sociological terms have been appropriated for propaganda purposes in the past few years, and used in a sense directly opposite to the original meaning. The sociological (and everyday) term 'institutional', for example, referred to what was specified exactly as the aims of the organisation, what the organisation's rules were, and what the organisation openly punished and rewarded. It now means the opposite. 'Institutional racism', for example, now means what is *unintended* by the organisation, what is 'hidden', what is 'unwitting', what is 'unconsciously' present in the minds of the organisation's members. 'Pluralism' has suffered similar inversion of its original meaning. Of course, sociology has no copyright on the English language. But current aspirations towards 'pluralism' must not be supposed to be aspirations towards pluralism in the old sense.

'Pluralism' now means a state of affairs in which, so to speak, *no* group 'fights its corner'. *No* individual attributes to his own hard-won or casually acquired opinions any superiority (or inferiority) over any other. To do so is regarded as a serious offence against 'pluralism' in the new sense.

To embrace ideas and ideals unless I *do* think they are the best or better than others is to do something that is literally nonsensical and meaningless. If they are not embraced because they do seem to me at this time to be 'more correct' or 'better' than others, why on earth should I embrace them at all?

The issue of what 'respect' means for those who believe in a pluralistic society in the old sense and those who believe in a pluralistic society in the new sense, a mass society, was well illustrated in the reaction to a call to the protestant Church of Ireland by the Roman Catholic Archbishop of Dublin, Desmond Connell (later Cardinal Connell) that the protestant Church of Ireland should not offer *protestant* Communion *to Roman Catholics*.[46]

If the protestant Church of Ireland were trying to make converts, that would be an expression of strong-group pluralism. But its action is based on mass-society pluralism—the belief that differences between Roman Catholic communion and Church of Ireland communion *do not matter*, they are of no importance.

The basis of old pluralistic ecumenism, as distinct from mass-society ecumenism, was to allow one's opponents to have their own estimate of what belief was important, for so long as they regarded it as important. It was not ecumenical in the strong-group, pluralistic, sense of ecumenism to ride rough-shod over that belief until such time as the opponent came to one's own view that the belief was *unimportant*. True *respect* was an acknowledgement of the importance an opponent places on a belief, until he or she could be peacefully persuaded to change it.

An editorial in the Dublin-based *Irish Independent* took a typically 'mass-society' line on the matter. Archbishop Connell, in restating what the rules were for *his* members, had 'perturbed' leaders of *other* churches. Though subtly stated, the argument of the *Irish Independent* was that because the editor and the Church of Ireland *did not* regard as important a rule for Roman Catholics what the Roman Catholic church *did* regard as an important rule for Roman Catholics, then neither the adherents of the protestant Church of Ireland, nor the adherents of the Roman Catholic Church need ... respect it.[47]

The new mass-society 'pluralists' and new mass-society 'multi-culturalists' purport to be (and many no doubt genuinely believe that they are) describing and supporting a free society. *In fact* their 'freedom' excludes the greatest and most important freedom of all—to join with others to protect and spread the ideas and ideals that one thinks are better. And what is better for me *might* be better for other people as well. It is my duty to put the best case I can to them, to peacefully persuade them to change their opinions or their ways—and be ready to be persuaded by them.

For the new 'pluralist' and new 'multi-culturalist', therefore, the 'mass society' is not a threat but an ideal. In their ideal mass society, all individuals are totally entitled to, and are sovereign over, their own beliefs and opinions—but over *only* their own opinions. They are not entitled to have adverse opinions about anybody else's beliefs and opinions. They are not entitled to organise with others to assert the superiority of their own beliefs and opinions.

John Hull, whose work has already been discussed in Chapter 2, was one of the most influential figures in post-1970 religious education in schools. It was not enough to respect the views of people with whom one disagreed, Hull wrote. It is necessary to *agree* with them intellectually and emotionally. 'We must learn to *share* each other's lives and to *participate* in each others hopes.'[48] The distinction between respect for a different opinion, and universal agreement on nothing in particular could not be more clearly enunciated.

By 2001 there was one belief, therefore, that was imperative, paramount and pervasive: the mass society was the good society. No credence could be given to the person who questioned that 'fact'; and no tolerance could be extended to the person who challenged that single, overriding value. Because of what Hitler did to the Jews, and because of what the British and Americans did to the African slaves, the worst term of contemporary abuse was 'racist', so the opponents of the mass society were now labelled ... racists.

Tocqueville foresaw long ago that extreme individualism could deteriorate into apathy and indifference, or into ignorant and intractable self-conceit, under whatever guise of 'tolerance' and 'equality'. Religious, political and social liberty would then slip away or be usurped. For that reason, he said, it was the duty of every person who valued it, without a faint heart, to 'keep watch and ward for freedom'.[49]

6

The Sociology of Post-1970 Religious Education

From 1870 to the 1950s in England the character of religious education in the state 'non-sectarian' schools was strongly influenced by the Church of England. During that period it occupied a privileged and important place in moulding and maintaining the nation's 'Christian culture'. The religious clauses of the 1944 Education Act were the work of William Temple, the Archbishop of Canterbury, who as Archbishop was well thought-of by the Conservative party, and as a Christian socialist of long standing was greatly admired by the Labour party. From 1944 the Church of England committee was one of the four committees that determined the content of the agreed syllabuses for religious education in the state schools of each locality.

But influence flowed the other way. The Church of England schools were not bound to follow the post-1944 agreed syllabuses, but they were more or less strongly affected by the thinking that surrounded them—that this was the way to teach religion to 'the children of today'. The 1960s proved a time of cultural upheaval, and after 1970 the influence of the modish secular ideas of the time about religious education in the state schools flowed ever more powerfully into Church of England thinking about how children in its own schools should be taught religion. The idea that they should be 'taught' the religious principles of the Church of England, 'taught' the Christian faith, or 'taught' religion at all, as anything to be accepted or believed, came increasingly to be regarded in both state and Church of England schools as undesirable and unacceptable 'indoctrination'.

In general, religious education came to mean the study of world religions. They were to be studied by the pupil not only without preconceptions of the superiority of one over the other, but also, in practice, with a ban on the notion that any one of them could be ever be considered as superior or inferior to any of the others. Called in aid of this type of religious education were the notion of 'value-free' phenomena (on the analogy of scientific objectivity), along with philosophical contributions, especially from 'phenomenology' and 'existentialism', bodies of thought that happened to be popular within the revolutionary student movements of the 1960s and early 1970s.

The Value-Free Study of Beliefs about Facts and Moral Values

The post-1970s 'value-free study of world religions' was heavily indebted to Max Weber's general conception of what sociology should be about, as well as to Weber's own comparative studies of religions.[1] It is perhaps fairer to Weber to say that it reflected some half-baked sociologists' idea of what Weber was saying.

Weber's general sociology, of which his sociology of religion was an application, was about 'understanding' given groups of people. What were their views of the present in terms of fact and morals? Crucially, what future state of affairs did they want to produce out of their present situation, as they perceived their present situation to be? *Perceptions* of situations and *intentions* as well as *actual* situations explain human conduct. The control perceptions and intentions exercised over human conduct, as distinct from mere reaction to present conditions, was what gave rise to the need for the special approach of the sociologist, anthropologist and psychologist in the scientific study of human beings. *Geisteswissenschaft,* the science of human conduct, had to add considerations of people's 'plans' to the armoury of *Naturwissenschaft*, the science of non-human nature.

What was or is *actually* true about their secular and spiritual situation, and what was or is *actually* good for them, were for Weber crucially important matters for study.

But neither the 'true' facts in general nor the 'valid' morals in general were the specialised business of the sociologist. The sociologist was interested in finding out what, as a matter of ascertained fact, people *believed* to be true and moral.

The sociologist's special business was the objective, value-free study of a given set of people's *'definitions of the situation'* (their present one, and the future one they are striving towards) in terms of their factual and moral perceptions. This is what constituted *verstehende Soziologie*, Weber's 'interpretative sociology'. *Wertfrei Soziologie*, was the objective, value-free study of subjectively-held values—of the values given people could be shown *empirically* to hold or to have held.

Weber's most celebrated applications of these recommendations were his studies of the Calvinist's view of God and His creation;[2] of the different 'definitions of the situation' held by the bureaucrat and the politician—for example, their different conceptions of 'honour'—the existence and integrity of which differences made constructive state activity possible;[3] and of the intellectual.[4] Ernst Troeltsch was an outstanding contemporary of Weber's who studied various types of Christian church and sect beliefs about ethics and politics in the Weberian manner.[5]

After Weber's death in 1920 other sociologists, especially under the title of 'the sociology of knowledge', took up his idea that sociology should be the study of what people *regard* as 'knowledge' of fact and value. Karl Mannheim's study of the typical conservative mentality (he labelled it 'ideological') as compared with the typical liberal mind-set (he labelled it as 'utopian') is one of the best-known examples.[6] Some of this work became a staple of the university teaching of sociology in America and Western Europe in the 1950s and 1960s.

Taking responsibility

Weber himself was not to the slightest degree a relativist. Nor was he an anarchist who saw no role for the state.[7] Say that to the best of his or her ability and resources a sociologist has objectively found out what a set of people *believes*

is true and virtuous, sacred and profane.[8] That does not
lessen the sociologist's responsibility, as a citizen, or in one
of his many other social capacities, to decide and state
publicly what on the best evidence available, to the best of
his or her knowledge, is his or her assessment of what is
true, and is his or her judgement of what is right. He or she
still has to make decisions on fact and value in the relevant
spheres of his or her life.

Weber clearly believed that there *are* better and worse
versions of both fact and value in relation to any situation
(not necessarily one's own version). When the sociologist
has done his or her value-free work, therefore, there
remains the equally important, or more important, task of
contributing his or her own best knowledge and value
judgement to the public debate, in order to improve the
general standards of social life. It was, for Weber, one's
responsibility to decide what was the best course of religious commitment, political policy, civic action and personal
conduct, in the light of the best facts and the soundest
ethics available at the time.

The sociologist must always be open to having his own
knowledge corrected, and having the moral judgements he
has made scrutinised and refined. Whether as spouse,
parent, neighbour, teacher, voter, politician, bureaucrat, it
was one's 'damned duty', Weber said, to take a moral stand
on the most reliable data.[9] Always open mindedly *seeking*
correction, it was one's duty to fight one's corner, until
satisfied that one's secular or religious 'facts' are wrong, or
that the moral principles one has been applying are invalid.

The value-free education of the young

Weber was particularly concerned about the abuse of their
position by certain professors in the pre-1914 Wilhelminian
Reich in inculcating into their students extreme nationalis-
tic opinions. The university teacher's task was to assist the
student to arrive at his own opinion of what was factually
correct about the natural world and supernatural forces,
and what was morally valid.

But nothing was further from Weber's own than the
standpoint that any one opinion was just as true and

morally valid as any other, and therefore it did not matter
what opinion the student formed. The university teacher's
task was to see to it that students *took seriously* the question of what was the best existing version of natural and
supernatural reality, and what was the most elevated body
of morals available at the time.

The student's own opinions had consequences; so did
other people's opinions have consequences. It followed,
therefore, that everybody had not only to take seriously his
own opinions and why he held them; he had to take everybody else's opinions seriously too. An 'education' that
resulted in the multi-faceted irresponsibility of relativism
and indifferentism was just as abhorrent to Weber as an
'education' that was a matter of coercive indoctrination. In
a remarkable peroration to his speech, 'Politics as a vocation', he prophesied accurately in 1918 what Germany
would look like within a few years, in making clear that he
believed the first, relativism, could easily result in the
second, tyranny.[10]

Weber discussed the roles of the university teacher and
the undergraduate. He did not discuss the roles of the
school teacher and the pupil but, *mutatis mutandis*, his
argument about taking choices seriously applies there too.
Perhaps it applies more strongly to the pupil than to the
student of university age and ability. The child of school age
is less able than the student to cope with a world in which
it has to make its own choices without firm guidance from
adults who care about them.

There are immense grey areas of uncertainty in all
science, theology and moral philosophy. Over all human
knowledge, and over all evaluations of conduct, there hangs
the permanent possibility of error. But that does not mean
that the teacher is properly a neutral spectator, or facilita-
tor, of the autonomous choices pupils make.

As a pedagogic *technique*, a technique *under the control
of the teacher*, leaving a child to 'find out for itself' has great
merits when applied over a vast range of experiences. The
child finds out for itself that if it rushes around too enthusi-
astically it will feel the pain of a bump or a graze. It discovers it is losing out if it continues to think that 2+2 = 3. It

discovers it is not understood by other people if it continues to think that the letters 'cat' signify an animal that barks. Where they are adverse for the child, that is, the consequences can be left by the teacher to do some of the teaching.

But, for example, the child does not discover for itself, until it is too late, that in the long run the psychotropic substances in some glues can have unpleasant consequences for itself and the people who have to look after it. The child might well discover, on the contrary, that the psychotropic substance give it transitory feelings of freedom and happiness.

In all such fields of human experience—of long-term risk to the individual and harm to other people, where self-indulgent pleasure, not pain, are nevertheless the short-term individual 'discovery'—the teacher is (ideally) the repository and transmitter of what has been discovered in the experience of many individuals in many societies, and by scientific and social-scientific investigation. In *these* fields, it is a misunderstanding and misapplication of a generally valuable educational practice to leave the child to 'clarify its own values', adopt its own strategy of 'harm reduction', and discover only after irrecoverable damage has been done what, after all, would have been 'right for itself'.

The teacher—the 'good' teacher—has something useful to pass on to children about those choices that generally prove prudent and those choices that generally prove dangerous; about wise and disastrous choices; about ignorance and knowledge; and about the way good people behave.

Uncertainty and error are the reasons for openness. The importance of being corrected is the justification for the difficult social achievement of tolerance. The belief that it does not matter if a person is corrected or not, because one view is just as good as any other, produces only the easy social attitudes of indifference and apathy, in a personal and social world composed of what in religious controversies used to be called 'adiaphora', things that 'don't matter'. Openness on the one hand and indifference on the other are often both referred to indiscriminately as 'tolerance'. But they are two types of tolerance of entirely different kinds, with entirely different origins and consequences. Obviously, *in practice*, and simply because of the enduring power of common sense, nearly all teachers in many school subjects recognise all this and act accordingly. But, since roughly 1970, relativism *in principle* has secured a firmer hold in educational theory and training for *social studies and religious studies* than every before. There is a post-1970s continuum. The teaching of languages lies near one extreme. Here there is some, but not much, scope for the teacher to act as a neutral chairperson, as each pupil decides for himself or herself whether the masculine third person singular of *être* is or is not *il est*, or whether what we call a pencil is or is not called *ein Bleistift* in German, and whether or not *Bleistift* is masculine, feminine or neuter. Near the other extreme is post-1970s religious studies.

The 'open society'

Weber was a great admirer of English liberty—and during the Great War, in Germany, a courageous one.[11] He would have abhorred the incorporation into religious education in schools of the mutations of his interpretative sociology and sociology of religion in three of its aspects.

His first objection would have been that the point of studying different conceptions of the world and of spiritual reality is to show the effects of those differences. The tendency of multi-faith courses as taught in the schools is to show that there are no significant differences—what was *important* about Religion was what was *common* to all religions. This was the case put by, for example, the theologian Professor John Hick in *The Myth of Christian Uniqueness*.[12]

The second objection that can be deduced from Weber's work is one of deep-seated moral principle His sociology could as well have been called *Verantwortungssoziologie*, the sociology of social responsibility, as *verstehende Soziologie*, the sociology of understanding.

For Weber, a person and an organisation had to take personal and group responsibility for finding the best set of facts, the best set of morals, the best religious faith that he, she or it could find, in good faith, through serious study, and with a mind open to correction. But people are not only responsible for their own views. People are responsible for playing their part in seeing to it that as many other people as possible hold as correct a view of the facts as possible and as sound morals as possible. No one stands above the constant necessity of having his or her view corrected—or transformed—by persuasive argument or example. In the long run no society is helped if it accepts the view that one person's beliefs and attitudes are just as good as any other person's.

Relativism helps no one to approach closer to the factual, moral or spiritual truth. For Weber, 'respect for other people and their opinions' meant they were important enough to be taken seriously. They might be better than one's own. They might be worse than one's own. Either way they had consequences for good or ill.

The Chief Rabbi, Jonathan Sacks, touched on this problem in his BBC Reith Lectures of 1990.

> The problem is that giving many religions equal weight is not supportive of each, but instead tends to relativise them all. It produces a strange hybrid in which *the primary value is personal choice.* ... That is a little like gluing together slices of Leonardo, Rembrandt, Van Gogh and Picasso and declaring the result the best in Western art.[13]

A successful society, in Weber's view, was not one whose members lacked the courage of their own convictions. It was not one whose members were indifferent to the convictions of others. It was one in which convictions were arrived at and changed by free discussion. It was one in which no one was coerced into joining any organisation if he or she did not agree with its means or ends. No one was prevented from leaving an organisation with whose means or ends he or she had come to disagree.

This approach to the differences that exist among individuals and cultural and religious groups has nothing to do, therefore, with a squeamish fear of contradicting others. Even less was it a licence for silencing someone who *does* hold and express an opinion in reasoned debate.

The third of Weber's objections was also implicit in all his work. Superficial study by the outsider, *à la carte*, of a way of looking at the world as profoundly important for believers as their religion, could not produce either knowledge or understanding. In his courteous, academic German, he condemned any such approach as *Dilettantismus*— irresponsible, uncommitted, frivolous dabbling. Knowing something about one great book was infinitely preferable to knowing next to nothing about each of a large number of great (or mediocre) books.

The readiness to work seriously on one's own world-view, to take seriously the world-view of another person or group; *the readiness to contest it if necessary*; and the institutional framework within which all this could and did happen— these things in unison Karl Popper called 'the open society'.[14]

The successful exponents of the new religious studies rarely appealed to the work of Max Weber, the implacable enemy of relativism in fact and value. They referred, rather, to a predecessor of Weber, Edmund Husserl. Husserl's existentialist philosophy was in harmony with the relativist ideas and ideals that came to be called 'post-modernism'. Rather than saying that the new approach to religious education in the schools was sociological (sociology had fallen into some discredit academically by the late 1970s) the new religious studies were said to be 'phenomeno-logical'.[15]

The 'Phenomenological' Approach to Religious Education in Schools

It is difficult to conceive of a more obscure, self-centred and pessimistic basis than phenomenology for the religious, not to speak of the Christian, education of children. It is a strangely antiquated basis for 'modern' religious education.. Phenomenology is a late-nineteenth-century and early-twentieth-century German 'philosophy', developed in particular by Edmund Husserl.

Husserl's phenomenology was a reaction against the distinctively late-nineteenth-century mechanistic and materialistic psychology that assimilated the study of human beings to the study of inanimate objects. Phenomenology, in contrast, presented itself as a method of investigating the peculiarities of being human. It fed into a philosophy that became much better known to the general public—existentialism. Existentialism itself took a distinct militantly atheistic as well as a Christian form.

The atheistic form sees the human being as purely a creature of this earth, whose only certainty is its own death. The central fact of life is its 'nothingness' (in French existentialism, *le Néant*; in German existentialism *das Nichts*) and the resulting all-pervasive anxiety. To live authentically is fully to grasp these two facts, and having done so, to create one's own being by acts of purely personal decision. By making these purely personal, 'authentic' decisions, one creates one's own character.

Christian existentialism was inspired by Søren Kierkegaard—again, not a modern, but a nineteenth-century thinker (born 1813, died 1855). It tests every Christian doctrine by its derivation from human experience. It 'demythologises' the Bible. Christian existentialism was condemned by Pope Pius XII in his encyclical *Humani generis* of 1950.

During the turbulent 1960s, these were the doctrines (or versions of them, or a *mélange* of them and other doctrines) that by historical accident happened to be fashionable among progressive intellectuals, and especially among leading student radicals and revolutionaries who read similar doctrines into Karl Marx's *Economic and Philosophical Manuscripts of 1844*. What grasp any particular adherent had of Husserl's, Sartre's, Heidegger's, Kierkegaard's, or Marx's actual work could have been established only by investigation. But by 1970 these philosophies, in one crude or refined form or another, filled the vacuum that had been created in religious education in schools.

Since the early 1970s reference has often been made in the literature to the importance of the 'phenomenological' approach to religious education in schools, and in that connection the work of Edmund Husserl is often cited. What is Husserl's philosophy?[16]

Edmund Husserl

Husserl had summarised his ideas for English-speaking audiences in an article in the *Encyclopaedia Britannica* in 1929. In 1931, his full position was made clear to them in the first English edition of his *Ideas: general introduction to pure phenomenology* and his Preface to it.[17]

He sought, he wrote, to 'found a new science'. The 'whole course of philosophical development since Descartes' had been preparing the way, Husserl wrote, for Husserl. This 'exclusive new scientific field' was what Husserl called 'Transcendental Subjectivity'.[18] Husserl claimed that Transcendental Subjectivity aimed at making philosophy a 'rigorous science'.

Transcendental Subjectivity, he said, demanded 'the *radical* attitude of *autonomous self-responsibility*'.[19] In his description of what he means by this Transcendental Subjectivity, Husserl produces his own way of looking at the world. *It is one of the most self-centred, and therefore one of the most relativistic, that has ever been produced in the history of thought.* I am the master, I am the mistress, of all external reality. *I* know what is 'real' by 'reflecting upon *myself*'. I focus consistently and exclusively upon that which is purely inward, upon what is 'phenomenologically' accessible to me. I possess in myself a self-contained, 'essential individuality', to which *all* 'real and objectively possible' experience and knowledge 'belongs'. Through the agency of this essential individuality—something that I become conscious of by focusing *exclusively* on *myself*—'the objective world is there *for me* with all its empirically confirmed facts'. It has *'for me at any rate'* 'trustworthy essential validity *(even if never scientifically authorised)*'.

> *I am the Ego* who invests the being of the world which I so often speak about with *existential validity*, as an existence which wins for me from *my own life's pure essence* meaning and essential validity.[20]

'Responsibility' is necessarily something exercised by some 'self'. But it normally means the responsibility of some 'self' to do something or have done something for *other* people, in the way that *other* people require. 'Autonomous self-responsibility', as the phrase is used by Husserl, is therefore near to being, if it is not entirely, an oxymoron.

The beauty of Husserl for anybody who wants to use him to justify their religious education in schools is that he provides a set of impressive-sounding formulations that need a great deal of effort to master, and arguments about them can always be made to run into the sand.

Husserl and phenomenology in relation to religious education in schools

As an 'approach' to religious education in schools, phenomenology emerged in the late sixties and was popular in the 1970s.[21] The 'phenomenological approach' to religious 'phenomena', Chater writes, is to study them 'neutrally' and 'without presuppositions'. Phenomenology 'as a method' is 'parallel to some forms of religious meditation'.[22] What a strange remark. Religious meditation is aimed at eliminating preoccupation with one's self and one's own consciousness, in order to contemplate the sacred and sublime —intent, like St. Herbert on his Derwentwater island, to adore the Deity with undistracted mind, and meditate on everlasting things. *Religious* meditation concentrates on the Absolute *Other*. *Phenomenological* meditation concentrates on the Absolute *Ego*.

Chater gives the following account of Husserl and phenomenology. 'In order to perceive *the universal* directly we must *remove the existing world* and any part of it and redirect our attention to the phenomena of consciousness.' (In Husserl's account of Transcendental Subjectivity that means one's *own* consciousness.) 'After this we must bracket out particulars so that the universal can be directly intuited. By this process, Husserl claims, we have access to the "essential forms constraining human existence".'[23]

A founder of the phenomenology that was popular in religious-education circles in the 1970s was Gerardus van der Leeuw. He writes:

> No judgement is expressed concerning the objective world ... All phenomena, therefore, are considered solely as they are presented to the mind, without any further aspects such as the real existence

or their value being taken into account. In this way the observer restricts himself to pure description systematically pursued, himself adopting the attitude of complete intellectual suspense or of abstention from all judgement, regarding these controversial topics.[24]

'The phenomenological or world religions approach' is thus based, Chater says, 'upon the attempt to help the child to understand religious commitment from the inside without any assumptions about the child's belief world.'[25] Pupils are to 'enter imaginatively and sympathetically into the experience of religious believers'—that is, of *other* religious believers.

The world religions are analysed against a 'check list' of 'seven dimensions': 'practical and ritual', 'experiential and emotional', 'narrative or mythic', 'doctrinal and philosophical', 'legal and ethical', 'social and institutional' and 'material'.[26]

The Westhill Project's package for religious education in schools, *How Do I Teach RE?*, identifies three main areas of content:[27]

- Traditional belief systems. These are said to be 'exemplified' in 'personal life, family life, public life, and communal life' and are 'observed' in 'symbols, stories and people';

- Shared human experiences. These are 'exemplified' 'likewise' and are 'observed' 'by looking at' 'answers to the crucial question': 'What does it mean to be human?';

- Individual patterns of belief. These are 'exemplified' 'in the same areas', though 'the way in which individual patterns of belief emerge in the classroom, and become material for exploration is entirely informal and *ad hoc*'.[28]

'Religious concepts are intended to emerge from the kinds of questions children ask about matters of importance ... .' This intention does not preclude 'some sort' of 'guidance' about 'recognised' theological 'conceptual systems'.[29] Two sets of concepts within such conceptual systems are identified. 'The first set includes concepts within traditional belief systems like "salvation", "God", "faith", and "spirituality", that belong to all religious *or non-religious* systems and, above this, are concepts specific to particular religions.' 'The second set of concepts is found within human experience and relates to "authority", "destiny", "meaning" and "value".'

The essential thing is to have the pupil experience these things 'phenomenologically'. These 'concepts' should be 'acquired' by 'skills of investigation and inquiry'. One of the best ways of helping children to explore these concepts ('God', 'salvation', 'destiny', 'meaning', 'value', etc.) is to 'present them with situations' where they 'encounter them at first hand'.

'Phenomenological' is such a mysterious term that it was used in all sorts of ways—so long as it labelled and justified the relativistic and ego-centred religious education of pupils. It was often used in the opposite sense to the extreme inwardness of Husserl's phenomenology, to mean the study of 'phenomena' in the way that word is often used loosely in everyday conversation—the study of objects, places and events.

These 'phenomenological methods' claimed to give pupils the ability to 'remove' particular examples of religion, in order to be able to see universal forms. All religions are expressions of the same divine reality. Religion, with a capital letter, can therefore be grasped by studying what 'religions' do with 'water', 'food', 'light', 'ritual', 'priesthood', 'pilgrimage' and so forth. This gives all religions 'unity'.

Such a programme of religious education would, therefore, have the additional benefit of making the children more 'tolerant' and 'empathic'.[30] It would contribute to multicultural education.[31]

Another 'crucial' advantage was that it enabled children to *work out their own beliefs*. The 'praiseworthy intention' of 'the informal and *ad hoc* nature of the emergence of *individual* patterns of belief' was to 'stop adults imposing their religious concepts on children'.[32] It did not 'make assumptions' about 'the personal commitments' of children—that is, it did not make assumptions about what the personal commitments of the pupils eventually, 'desirably' (from the point of view of the pupil's family, school or society) should be.

'Experiential' or 'Affective' Religious Education in Schools

From the late 1970s the 'varieties of religious *experience*', to use William James' famous phrase,[33] began to attract more attention.

Reports from the Religious Studies Research Centre (founded by the Professor of Zoology at Oxford, Sir Alister Hardy) began to appear. The purpose of the Centre was to investigate the nature and frequency of these 'religious experiences'. They concerned such things as one's *own unique* personal religious *feelings*, such as sensing 'a presence', a personal sense of harmony with nature, a personal sense of profound joy with nature, a personal sense of the presence of the dead, a premonition, a personal sense of a meaning in the pattern of events, a personal sense of God's presence, the belief that a prayer had been answered, and the feeling of having been converted.[34]

Growing discomfort with the 'take-it-or-leave-it' approach of the sociology of religion in its—alleged—Husserlian guise, and the difficulty of teaching religion in schools phenomeno-logically, made it possible for this so-called 'experiential approach' to make headway in the 1980s.[35]

The experiential approach in schools is less the academic study of religion than an attempt to let religion appeal to children. It 'wishes to allow children' to develop their *own* 'religiosity'.

This emphasis was built into several locally-agreed syllabuses, in which 'attainment outcomes' were to be accomplished by the 'personal search of the individual' in 'exploring emotional, affective and relational areas', 'some-times known as right-brain activity'.[36]

Religion was looked on favourably, in this highly general-ised sense of 'religion'. In 1995 a discussion paper issued by the School Curriculum and Assessment Authority (SCAA) argued that spiritual and moral development was impor-tant. It ought to be fostered. It should not be simply a school subject. It should be an integral part of the ethos of the school. 'Spiritual development' included the development of 'awe, wonder, awareness of transcendence, ... and aware-

ness of ultimate questions'.[37] Spiritual and moral development was about 'expressing meaning', 'relationships',
'ultimate questions', and 'personal understanding'.

What is RE?, published by the British Council of
Churches Religious Education Consultants' Group and the
Christian Education Movement (CEM), recommends that
syllabuses should enable pupils to develop the capacity of
reflection on *themselves*. They should reflect on their
experiences of wonder, failure, death, and birth. Themes
should be explored in different faiths: water, fire, religious
locations.[38]

Although it is 'religious', it is as ego-centred as is the
so-called 'phenomenological approach' to religious education. Pupils imagine themselves to be something, 'perhaps
a car or a piece of fruit or other object'. The purpose is to
allow pupils to begin to 'embody awareness'. Each pupil is
to learn to 'value' (i.e. highly value) its *own* personal
experience. Pupils are asked to compare with other pupils
the kind of things they have imagined themselves to be. By
this means each pupil will be brought to realise that
experience differs from person to person, from body to body.
Pupils thus develop the skills by which they can both
recognise 'different perspectives' and (yet again) 'empathise'
with them.

It is also relativistic, in that it emphasises the equal
validity of all 'experiences'. As in phenomenological religious education, the message is that differences between
religions are trivial. Religion, again with a capital letter, is
essentially a matter of the 'numinous' in all religions, the
sense of reverence *felt* by the *individual*. Christianity is
merely a variation on this theme.

Existentialists like Jean-Paul Sartre argue that each
person is distinctively human only by making choices, and
through the choices he or she makes. 'I am what I chose to
be.' 'In choosing, I am free.' What matters in life is being
authentic, and being authentic means choosing according to
principles that must *not* be 'justified', that is, must *not*
require anybody else's approval. To have principles that are
held because others approve of them is to fall into the trap
of becoming 'a being-for-others'.

The experiential approach to religious education therefore buttressed the highly ego-centred 'values-clarification' approach to ethics in the schools pioneered by Abraham Maslow and Carl Rogers.[39]

The existential psychology of Rogers and Maslow, with its emphasis on 'person-centredness' (self-centredness not other-person centredness)—on each individual making his or her own personal choices, and each individual's own attempts to discover a satisfying sense of identity and meaning in life—secured a dominant place in teacher training from the late 1970s onwards (even though Rogers himself, in the light of what he regarded as its disastrous consequences, had in the meantime repudiated his own earlier work).[40]

Neither the multi-faith, nor the 'phenomenological', nor the experiential approaches were successful in producing pupils who knew much about Christianity—it was explicitly not the intention of the experiential approach, and not high on the agenda of the 'phenomenological' approach. In 1991 a MORI poll found that 57 per cent of 18-24 year olds could not say what Good Friday commemorated.[41] In 1994 Professor Thomas Barden said that he was shocked to find that his students at Swansea university did not know what the word the 'beatitudes' referred to.[42]

An anecdote: A lecturer at the University of Newcastle upon Tyne was talking to a school leaver who had followed such a syllabus. In the autumn of the year 2000 she was helping at her local university before going on to her own college. Somehow the question came casually into the conversation, 'Which are the four Gospels?' 'Matthew, John ... er, was it Luke?' 'Matthew, Luke, John and ...?' 'Er ... Was there somebody else?' 'Yes, there were four of them. Matthew, Luke, John and ...?' Finally she was told it was Mark's. Then she said, 'Are they in the Old Testament or the New?'

By 1985 only six per cent of maintained secondary schools were complying with their legal obligation to have a daily act of collective worship.[43] Hansard reported that in 1987 nearly two out of three fourth-year children received no

school religious education, Christian, multi-faith, phenomenological, experiential, or thematic.[44] Half the secondary
schools in Barking and Dagenham offered no religious
education in years four and five. The authority's agreed
syllabus was largely unknown by those teaching religious
education in the schools inspected.[45]

The Massive Judgements Inherent in this 'Non-judgementalism'

The temporary non-judgementalism of social scientific research

Students of society of the Max Weber type (rather than
'students' as pupils in a school) work in the light of an
hypothesis—what they might find, or even what they expect
to find. But they have no commitment to verifying their
hypothesis. On the contrary, in best practice they look
especially hard, like any scientist, for information that will
prove that their own hypothesis is wrong.

In carrying out work on other people's view of the world,
they are non-judgemental, too, for a practical reason that
does not enter the picture for the natural scientist. The
members of the group whose world-view they are studying
will not be very open to the investigator if he or she radiates
disapproval of what he or she is discovering.

The investigator of a group's world-view is ideally
non-judgemental for a third reason. Until he or she has
completed the investigation, the best information is still
lacking. As a result of the investigation—if it is indeed a
contribution to knowledge, and not either a failure or a
fraud—better comparisons will be capable of being made
with other groups of the scientific accuracy, coherence, or
practical utility of the group's world-view.

All along the line, then, judgement is suspended, not
until perfect data are available, not until perfect moral
insight is acquired, but until the best data, and the best
basis for moral judgement have to be utilised to meet the
demands of public policy and personal life.

*The permanent non-judgementalism of post-1970 religious
education*

The non-judgementalism of post-modernism and other
relativist philosophies is of an entirely different kind. It
presupposes that whatever group is studied, there will be
nothing *significant* in, there will be nothing *important*
about, its particular world-view and those of its constituent
organisations and individuals. The consequences in conduct
of their holding one factual, religious and moral view of the
world and the spirit rather than another may or may not be
the same as the consequences of holding a different view.
But whatever the beliefs, whatever the results of holding
those beliefs, it is all in the end 'six and two threes'. None is
or can be more accurate or better than any other.

That is the pervasive and permanent pre-judgement of
the relativist.

This doctrine has been successfully propagated as the
proper approach to 'religious education' in the schools. The
message is inculcated that what the pupil will find is that
all religions are equally acceptable or equally unacceptable.
The conclusion of equality-for-all-practical-purposes, and
therefore the absence of any basis for preference except
personal taste, *chacun à son goût*, is permanently drawn *for*
the pupil before the first lesson begins. 'Society', the
provider of the educational system, the teacher, the father,
the mother, have nothing to say about the decision as a good
one or a bad one, as better or worse than any other.

Another force behind the principled *permanent*
non-judgementalism of this approach to religion was
Marxism. To the Marxist, religions were all equally undesirable, except as temporary solace, as the opium of the people.
All were equally unimportant as the superficial product of
underlying economic forces. These would soon be the
economic forces of a communist society, and they would
render religion redundant.

Writers who approve of non-judgemental religious
education sometimes inadvertently *do* declare a judgement
—that religion as a serious belief is a mere relic from a

benighted past. The uncommitted study of world religions, rather than the committed study of Christianity, is a product of intellectual freedom 'born of the Enlightenment'. Thus, for example, the eighteenth-century Enlightenment is described as being 'in contrast to the perceived dogmatism of the middle ages and the religious warring of the sixteenth and seventeenth centuries'. The Enlightenment saw 'the emergence of a new, more human-centred way of understanding and approaching religion; this was the study of religions as expressions of the human quest for meaning, in contrast to the more traditional study of theology as *revealed truth*'.[46]

Relativism in religion in the schools was the intention, and it has been the result. But if the phenomenological approach is the correct approach to religion, it is also the correct approach to politics. How can one meaningfully respect a politician for the care he has taken to master his brief, and the integrity with which he has selected his goals and the means to attain them, when everybody's opinion on the matter is just as good as any other? If in religion, then in politics also, it all depends on your own self-chosen (curiously termed) 'perspective', which is neither better nor worse than anybody else's. If the phenomenological approach is correct in religion and politics, why is it not correct in university life? What is the point of laboriously collecting data in the social sciences, either as student or staff, if such data are no better than anybody's opinion?

In the 1950s and 1960s, knowledge about the diverse versions of the facts, and different views of morality, was most commonly regarded as a necessary tool in the hands of those who wanted to reduce the level of error and evil in the world (political parties, governments, social workers of many sorts, and churches).

In dealing with 'deviants' (as they were called in the 1950s and 1960s) it was necessary to start from where they were in their attitudes and conduct, *in order to move them to where they ought to be*. In dealing with children, education had to be child-centred. Again, the sole reason for this was that, by knowing where the child was coming from, it could be more effectively brought to where it ought to go. In the more extreme forms of Deweyism, the child was seen as more or less naturally arriving at some destination of good personal character and civic behaviour *of which the educator approved*.

As applied to fellow-citizens, the approach in an open society to other people's views and actions is to assume that reasoned argument in good faith is the only permissible means of fostering them or opposing them. Manipulation, no less than coercion, intimidation and lies are ruled out. In an open society people listen to an opponent's case with a readiness to be corrected. But they treat their opponent's case, in turn, as sufficiently important to seek to correct it, where they believe it to be factually distorted, or morally or spiritually mistaken. They treat both their own view of the world *and that of their opponent* seriously, that is to say, with respect. Such liberty has been, Lord Acton said, 'the soul of what is great and good in the progress of the last two hundred years'.[47]

Respect, in this sense, is neither necessary nor possible, it is simply irrelevant, if all views of the world are equally valid. If all views of the world are equally true and equally good, then one set of people can feel only indifference if the effects on them of the world-view of another set of people are neutral; pleasure if they are beneficial; and defiance, hatred, fear or helplessness if they are oppressive.

Of course, a person in an open society does not treat everything that is said and written by all opponents with the same degree of attention. He assumes that certain bodies of fact have been pretty well established as sound information; and certain kinds of behaviour have been pretty well established as benign morality.

No one could live by the rule that he or she will treat all statements of fact that somebody else makes as if each was as possibly true as any other (e.g. that the earth is, after all, flat). Nor could people live by the rule that they will treat all the actions of other people, and all the moral propositions they appeal to, as equally valid (e.g. that torturing somebody else if it gives you pleasure is, after all, morally good). Any such attempt would be utterly wasteful of energy. It is a human impossibility to accomplish it.

The Rev. David Holloway says that after a lecture to students at the University of Newcastle upon Tyne, he stated in answer to a question that he preferred the *political arrangements* of the West to the *political arrangements* prevailing in many Islamic countries.

> I said that I would rather live in Newcastle, where there was freedom for Christian churches *and for mosques*, than in Tehran under the mullahs. This public expression of preference was treated with horror by a number of students. One threatened to report me to the Race Relations Board.[48]

In this new scheme of intolerant liberty—passionately upheld on this occasion not by the most ignorant in society but by the best educated—everyone is permitted to hold any belief about data or morals they like, *except* the belief that they have good grounds for preferring, for the present, their version of the facts and morals to anybody else's. No one can be permitted to state or imply that, until their flaws are exposed by intellectual and spiritual labour and open-minded discussion, their factual and moral beliefs are 'better' than others, or even (God forbid!), 'the best'.

This common result was aimed at or approved by a wide range of otherwise diverse political and educational doctrines, especially in the forms in which they were propagated and absorbed during the cultural upheavals of the 1960s. The speed and completeness with which they conquered mass entertainment and moulded general standards of conduct may have been unexpected. But most unexpected of all was the assistance they were afforded, in a social process resembling assisted suicide, by their natural opponents, the religious establishment, who for 30 years looked on with innocent and benign approval as these fatal doctrines were preached even in their own schools.

Notes

Foreword

1   Tocqueville, Alexis de, *Democracy in America*, Vol. 2, p. 318.

2   Himmelfarb, G., *One Nation, Two Cultures*, New York: Vintage, 2001; Gitlin, Todd, *The Twilight of Common Dreams: Why America is Wracked by Culture Wars*, New York: Henry Holt, 1995.

1: State Subsidy and State Control

1   Churton, E. (ed.), *A Memoir of Joshua Watson*, London: J.H. and James Parker, 1864.

2   Brown, C.K.F., *The Church's Part in Education 1833-1941*, National Society and SPCK, 1942, pp. 11-12. Cited in Huelin, G., 'Innovation: the National Society 1811-1934', in Leonard, G. and Yates, J. (eds.), *Faith for the Future: essays on the Church in education to mark 175 years of the National Society*: London: National Society and Church House Publishing, 1986, p. 20. Gordon Huelin was archivist and librarian at the SPCK.

3   The National Society set up its own teacher training colleges. St Mark, Chelsea, was founded for men in 1841. Whiteland was founded for women, who had to follow the rules laid down by the National Society on 'simplicity of dress among the mistresses in training'. Battersea was founded as a college for training teachers especially for the mining and agricultural areas. In 1845 the National Society opened its own 'depository' where teachers and students could find books and other materials.

4   Garbett, C., *The Claims of the Church of England*, London: Hodder and Stoughton, 1947, p. 215.

5   *Report of the Parliamentary Committee on the Education of the Lower Orders in the Metropolis and Beyond*, 1816. The work of the committee had been promoted by Henry Brougham.

6   *Report of the Parliamentary Committee on the Education of the Lower Orders in the Metropolis and Beyond*, 1818.

7   Lord John Russell to Lord Lansdowne, 4 February
      1839.

8   Chadwick, O., *The Victorian Church*, London: A. and
      C. Black, 1970. I, p. 344. Cited in Huelin, *Faith for
      the Future*, 1986, pp. 23-24.

9   Sadler, M.E. and Edwards, J.W., 'Summary of
      statistics, regulations etc. of elementary education in
      England and Wales 1833-1870', in *Special Reports on
      Educational Subjects II*, 1898, p. 80. Throughout the
      mid-Victorian period there were schools
      unashamedly calling themselves the 'ragged schools'.
      The ragged school movement began in the early
      1840s. John Pounds, a Portsmouth cobbler, had
      collected ragged children together and tried to give
      them care and training. The idea was taken up,
      prominently by Lord Shaftesbury in the evangelical
      tradition, who in 1844 helped form the Ragged School
      Union. In 1870 the Ragged School Union was
      running 132 schools, catering for 25,000 children.
      Some were taken over by the School Boards, but even
      as late as 1887 there was a residuum for whom the
      ragged schools catered, for 'even Board school
      teachers do not like to take shoeless, shirtless and
      capless children into their schools'. (Cross
      Commission, *Third Report*, 1887, p. 439.) Lawson, J.
      and Silver, H., *A Social History of Education*,
      London: Methuen, 1973, p. 285.

10   Lawson and Silver, *Social History of Education*,
      1973, p. 269.

11   In 1843, a similar agreement was made with the
      Nonconformists' British and Foreign Society, that
      inspectors would not be appointed without the
      Society's agreement.

12   Rogers, J.E.T. (ed.), *Speeches on Questions of Public
      Policy by John Bright*, London: 1969, p. 530.

13   Baines, E., *The Social, Educational, and Religious
      State of the Manufacturing Districts*, London: 1843.
      Lawson and Silver, *Social History of Education*,
      1973, p. 275.

14   *State of Popular Education in England*, 1861, pp.
      293-96 and p. 300.

15 Hurt, J., *Education in Evolution: church, state, society and popular education 1800-1870*, London: Hart Davis, 1971, Chapter 7.

16 Sadler and Edwards, *Special Reports II*, 1898, p. 57.

17 'We have lived to hear the recantation of Miall and Baines—to hear them declare that ... voluntaryism is quite an inadequate basis for a national system.' *Report of the First General Meeting of the National Education League*, Birmingham: NEL, 1869. Cited in Lawson and Silver, *Social History of Education*, 1973, p. 275.

18 Walpole, S., *History of England*, I, 212. Cited in Hammond, J.L. and Hammond, B., *The Town Labourer 1760-1832: a new civilisation* (1917), Abingdon, Oxon: Fraser Stewart, 1995, pp. 55-56.

19 *Report of the Factory Commission*, 1834. Dr Mitchell's report, p. 46.

20 *Report of the Commission of Children's Employment*, 1842.

21 Cited in Hammond and Hammond, *Town Labourer*, 1995, pp. 55.

22 Hammond and Hammond, *Town Labourer*, 1995, p. 247.

23 Hammond and Hammond, *Town Labourer*, 1995, p. 248. On Cobbett's views on schools, and his own achievements as a self-educator and a 'home school' educator, see Dennis, N. and Halsey, A.H., *English Ethical Socialism: St Thomas More to R.H. Tawney*, Oxford: Clarendon, 1988.

24 The 'Board' schools until 1902, the 'council' schools until 1944, the 'county' schools after that.

25 *Education of the Adolescent*, London: HMSO, October 1926. The Board of Education's guidance on the creation of separate primary and senior departments was given in its pamphlet, *The New Prospect in Education*.

26 Holtby, R., 'Duality: the National Society 1934-1986', in Leonard, G. and Yates, J. (eds.), *Faith for the Future: essays on the Church in education to mark 175 years of the National Society*: London: The

National Society and Church House Publishing, 1986, p. 27.

27 *White Paper on Educational Reconstruction*, London: HMSO, July 1943.

28 Cited in Garbett, *The Claims of the Church of England*, 1947, p. 216.

29 Evans, J.A., *Twelve Talks on Christian Citizenship*, London: Educational Interim Committee of the Christian Social Council, the Council of Churches in England for Social Questions, no date (1930?), p. 64.

30 Garbett, *Claims of the Church of England*, 1947, pp. 215-17.

31 Home Office, *Criminal Statistics England and Wales*, London: HMSO, annually. Dennis, N., *The Invention of Permanent Poverty*, London: ISCS, 1997, p. 66.

32 Under the 1944 Act primary schools had managers, secondary schools had governors. Governors had more powers than managers. From 1980 all schools were governed. There were further changes in the 1986 Act.

33 The National Society, *The Fourth R*, (Durham report), London: The National Society and SPCK, 1970, p. 255.

34 Dent, H.C., *The Education Act 1944*, London: London University Press, 1944.

35 *Crisis in the Church Schools*, London: The National Society and General Synod Board of Education, 1972.

36 Successive officers of the Society were 'deeply indebted' to him. Holtby, 'Duality: the National Society 1934-1986', 1986, p. 29.

37 DfEE, *School Governors: a guide to the law*, London: DfEE, 1994. Duncan, G. and Lankshear, D.W., *Church Schools: a guide for governors,* London: The National Society, 1996.

38 Under section 259 of the 1993 Education Act, it was made clear that section 13 of the 1992 Act meant that the denominational inspector must inspect the school's collective worship, as well as its religious education syllabus.

39 Brown, A. and Lankshear, D.W., *Inspection Hand-book: for section 13 inspections in schools of the Church of England*, London: The National Society, 1995.

40 *The 1999 Report of the European School Survey Project on Alcohol and Other Drugs (ESPAD)*, Edinburgh: Alcohol and Health Research Centre, February 2001.

41 Chrisafis, A., 'Everyone we know is desperate for pills', *Guardian*, 21 February 2001.

42 Office for National Statistics, 'Report: conceptions in England and Wales 1997', *Population Trends 95*, Spring 1999, pp. 51-52.

43 Marie Stopes International, 24 May 2001, (www.mariestopes.org.uk).The MSI web site and press release both quote Dr Parry's praise of the 'responsible' sexual intercourse of school children age 16 and younger on supervised school trips as being based on her astonishing though mistaken assumption that one quarter of *all* 16 year olds and younger on supervised school trips had engaged on such a trip in unprotected full sexual intercourse. Dr Parry is quoted as saying that 'A quarter of *respondents* didn't use any contraception at all and put themselves at risk of contracting sexually transmitted infections and experiencing crisis pregnancies. If these findings are reflected nationally, a quarter *of young people on school trips* having unprotected sex is a real cause for concern.' See also Marie Stopes International, *Your Passport to Sexual Health*, London: MSI, May 2001.

44 National Children's Bureau.

45 Allison, R. and Hall, S., 'Battle to cut teenage pregnancy rate', *Guardian*, 22 February 2001. Emphasis added.

46 Department for Education and Employment, *Schools: Building on Success*, London: DfEE, 2001.

2: Christianity in State Schools

1   Pope Gregory's answers to St Augustine's nine
      questions, received by St Augustine in AD 601, can be
      seen as an early example of 'religious education'.
      Bede, *A History of the English Church and People* (AD
      731), Harmondsworth: Penguin, 1968, pp. 74-83.

2   *Liber Decretalium Gregorii IX*, III, I, 3.

3   Lawson, J. and Silver, H., *A Social History of
      Education in England*, London: Methuen, 1973,
      p. 37.

4   Wood, N., *The Reformation and English Education: a
      study of the influence of religious uniformity on
      English education in the sixteenth century*, London:
      Routledge, 1931, p. 170.

5   Lawson and Silver, *Social History of Education*,
      1973, p. 101. During Elizabeth's reign the
      universities were gradually converted into
      strongholds of the new state religion. At Oxford, from
      1563 all graduands had to subscribe to the
      Thirty-nine Articles. From 1581 this applied to all
      undergraduates over the age of sixteen. Oxford was
      therefore closed to any but Anglicans. It was largely
      in the interests of *religious* discipline and uniformity
      that all Oxford students were finally made to reside
      in college or hall. From 1616 an ordinance of James I
      required recipients of degrees at Cambridge as well
      as Oxford to subscribe to the Royal Supremacy, the
      Book of Common Prayer, and the Thirty-nine
      Articles. (These religious 'tests', as they were called,
      which restricted admission to Oxford and Cambridge
      to members of the Church of England, were not
      finally removed until 1871.) Lawson and Silver,
      Social History of Education, 1973, p. 102.

6   Lawson and Silver, *Social History of Education*,
      1973, p. 179.

7   Lawson and Silver, *Social History of Education*,
      1973, p. 215. Emphasis and punctuation as in
      original.

8   Johnson, R.B., *The Letters of Hannah More*, London:
      1925, p. 183.

9   Lawson and Silver, *Social History of Education,*
    1973, p. 240.

10 Lawson and Silver, *Social History of Education,*
    1973, p. 231.

11 Cited in Brown, F.K., *Fathers of the Victorians,*
    Cambridge: Cambridge University Press, 1961, p. 76.

12 Trevelyan, G.M., *English Social History: a survey of
    six centuries from Chaucer to Queen Victoria* (1942),
    London: Penguin, 1986, p. 494.

13 Alfred, Lord Tennyson, 'Idylls of the King: the coming
    of Arthur', *The Poems of Alfred, Lord Tennyson
    1857-1869,* London: Dent, no date. My copy shows
    that it was a class prize in July 1913.

14 Churton, E. (ed.), *A Memoir of Joshua Watson,*
    London: J.H. and James Parker, 1864.

15 *Statement to the Inhabitants of Kennington, South
    Lambeth ... Disposed to Assist in the Instruction of the
    Infant Poor,* 1823. Cited in Lawson and Silver, *Social
    History of Education,* 1973, p. 243.

16 *Report of the Parliamentary Committee on the
    Education of the Lower Orders,* 1818. Emphasis
    added.

17 *Report of the Parliamentary Committee on the State of
    Education,* 1834, pp. 69-70.

18 *Committee on the State of Education,* 1834,
    pp. 220-25.

19 Brontë, C., *Shirley: a tale* (1850), London: Penguin,
    1994, chap. XVII.

20 Lawson and Silver, *Social History of Education,*
    1973, p. 271. Emphasis added.

21 *Minutes of the Committee of Council 1840-41,* p. 437.
    Cited in Lawson and Silver, *Social History of
    Education,* 1973, pp. 271-72.

22 Montague, C.J., *Sixty Years of Waifdom: or the
    ragged school movement in English history* (1904),
    London: Murray, 1969, p. 37. Mann, H., *Education in
    Great Britain: being the official report of H. Mann,*
    London: Census Office, 1854, p. lxv.

23   *Report of the Commissioners appointed to inquire into the State of Popular Education in England,* (Newcastle Commission), London: HMSO, 1861, pp. 343-44. Emphasis added.

24   Briggs, J. and Sellers, I. (eds.), *Victorian Nonconformity: documents of modern history,* London: Arnold, 1973, pp. 136-37.

25   The National Education League was opposed by the National Education Union, emanating from Manchester, representing Anglicans and Conservatives.

26   Forster, W.E., in a speech introducing the 1870 Elementary Education Bill, 17 February 1870. Forster was a Radical and a Quaker. His brother-in law was the school inspector, social commentator and poet, Matthew Arnold, who was himself, of course, the son of the great reforming headmaster of Rugby, Thomas Arnold. Matthew Arnold and Forster were both concerned with the emerging problem, as they saw it, of how 'civilisation' could be secured in a society where the sea of Faith was steadily ebbing, with its long, melancholy, withdrawing roar, 'down the dark edges drear, and naked shingles of the world'. (Arnold, 'Dover Beach'.)

27   *The Army and Religion: an enquiry into its bearing upon the religious life of the nation,* London: Macmillan, 1919, p. 113. The copy in the Robinson Library, Newcastle upon Tyne belonged to the famous left-wing economist J.A. Hobson (1858-1940) a circumstance that is indicative of the seriousness with which Christianity was taken by the Labour party in those days.

28   Garrett, C., *Loving Counsels: sermons and addresses,* London: Woolmer, 1887. Cited in Briggs and Sellers, *Victorian Nonconformity,* 1973, p. 137.

29   *Kama Sutra of Vātsyāyana* (translated by Burton, R. and Arbuthnot, F.F.) (1883), New Delhi: Arnold-Heinemann, 1982.

30   Briggs and Sellers, *Victorian Nonconformity,* 1973, pp. 134-36.

31   *Report of the Royal Commission on the Elementary*
      Education Acts (Cross report), 1888, part IV, pp.
      122-27. Emphasis added.

32   Smith, F., *A History of Elementary Education*
      1760-1902, London: University of London Press,
      1931, p. 326.

33   *Elementary Code,* 1904. This introduction is
      sometimes attributed to Sir Robert Morant, but it
      has also been suggested that it was written by J.W.
      Mackail, a civil servant in the Education Department
      1884-1919, and Professor of Poetry at Oxford.

34   Fisher, H.A.L., in a speech introducing the Education
      Bill, 10 August 1917. Fisher was a distinguished
      historian.

35   *Report of the Consultative Committee of the Board of*
      Education on the Education of the Adolescent,
      (Hadow report), London: HMSO, 1926, Introduction,
      pp. xix-xxii. Emphasis added.

36   John Dewey (1859-1952). Dewey was professor of
      philosophy at the universities of Michigan, Chicago
      and Columbia. He was influenced by, and became
      one of the most influential exponents of, the
      philosophy of 'pragmatism' of William James and of
      C.S. Peirce.

37   Dewey, J., *The Child and the Curriculum*, and *The*
      School and Society (1899), Chicago: University of
      Chicago, 1902. Dewey, J., *The School and*
      Society(1916) *etc.,* New York: Macmillan, 1961.

38   Lawson and Silver, *Social History of Education,*
      1973, p. 398. There were three Hadow reports, one on
      the education of the adolescent (1926), the second on
      the primary school (1931), the third on the infant and
      nursery school (1933). The Committee chaired by
      Will Spens reported on secondary education in the
      grammar and technical schools in 1938.

39   Wordsworth, W., 'Childhood and school-time', *The*
      Prelude (1799), in *The Works of William Wordsworth,*
      Ware: Wordsworth editions, 1994, p. 638 and p. 641.

40   Smith, *History of Elementary Education*, 1931, p.
      324.

41   Kekewich, G.W., *The Education Department and After*, London: Constable, 1920.

42   'Introduction', *Report of the Consultative Committee of the Board of Education*, (Hadow report), London: HMSO, 1931, pp. xvii-xxix in Maclure, J.S., *Educational Documents England and Wales 1816-1967*, 2nd edn, London: Methuen, 1968.

43   *Report of the Consultative Committee of the Board of Education*, 1931, pp. 92-93.

44   *Report of the Consultative Committee of the Board of Education*, 1931, pp. xvii-xxix.

45   Dent, P., *A New Approach to the Church's Work with Growing Boys and Girls*, London: The National Society, 1938.

46   Temple, W., 'Presidential address to the National Society' (1942), in Temple, W., *The Church Looks Forward*, London: Macmillan, 1984. p. 52. Emphasis added.

47   Temple, W., *Citizen and Churchman*, London: Eyre and Spottiswoode, 1941, pp. 25-26.

48   Temple, *Citizen and Churchman*, 1941, p. 12.

49   Temple, *Citizen and Churchman*, 1941, pp. 35-37. Emphasis added.

50   Temple, *Citizen and Churchman*, 1941, pp. 26-27.

51   Temple, *Citizen and Churchman*, 1941, pp. 27-28.

52   'Preface', *The Book of Common Prayer ... According to the Use of the Church of England*: Oxford: Oxford University Press, no date.

53   *Hansard*, 397, 2397.

54   *Hansard*, 397, 2396.

55   *Hansard*, 397, 2410.

56   *Hansard*, 397, 2433.

57   *Hansard*, 397, 2437. Emphasis added.

58   Part II, section 7.

59 Part II, section 25 of the 1944 Act is headed
'Religious Education in County and Voluntary
Schools'. Para. 1: 'The school day in every county
school and in every voluntary school shall begin with
collective worship.' Para. 2: 'Religious instruction
shall be given in every county school and in every
voluntary school.' The remaining paragraphs of
Section 25 deal with conscientious withdrawal of
children, and alternative religious instruction for
them. Section 26: 'In county schools religious
instruction shall be given in accordance with the
agreed syllabus, which shall not include any
catechism or formulary which is distinctive of any
particular religious [sic not 'Christian'']
denomination.'

60 Hansard, 397, 2426. Emphasis added.

61 House of Lords Official Report (Hansard), 21 June
1944, col. 368. Emphasis added.

62 House of Lords Official Report (Hansard), 11 July
1944, cols. 778 and 781.

63 House of Lords Official Report (Hansard), 11 July
1944, col. 778.

64 The Bristol syllabus of 1960 reads: 'founded securely
on the Bible it reaches out to the needs of young
people in every part of their lives, not hesitating to
relate the teaching of Jesus Christ to the problems of
the world as the child sees them'. The Birmingham
syllabus of 1962 says: 'when we speak of religious
education we mean Christian education'. The aim
was 'quite simply to confront children with Jesus
Christ'.

65 Curtis, S.J. and Boultwood, M.E.A., *An Introductory
History of English Education Since 1800*, 4th edn,
London: University Tutorial Press, 1966, pp. 413-14.
Emphasis added. Curtis drew up the details of the
1947 syllabus.

66 Chater, M., 'Philosophy of religious education', in
Kay, W.K and Francis, L.J. (eds.), *Religion in
Education*, Vol. I, Leominster, Herefordshire:
Gracewing, 1997, p. 258.

67 Chater, *Religion in Education*, Vol. I, 1997, p. 258.

68   Holtby, R.T., 'Duality: the National Society
     1934-1986', in Leonard, G. and Yates, J. (eds.), *Faith
     for the Future: essays on the Church in education to
     mark 175 years of the National Society*: London: The
     National Society and Church House Publishing,
     1986, p. 33. Robert Holtby was general secretary of
     the National Society (1967-74), and first joint general
     secretary of the National Society and the General
     Synod Board of Education (1974-1977). He was made
     Dean of Chichester in 1977.

69   *Half Our Future: a report of the Central Advisory
     Council for Education*, (Newsom report), London:
     Central Advisory Council for Education (England),
     August 1963, Chapter 7. Emphasis added. The
     Lancashire syllabus of 1973 (adopted also by
     Northumberland) reflected the approach of the
     Newsom committee. It states that 'in a country whose
     culture and traditions have received the deep
     impress of Christianity, it is an inescapable duty to
     help them find out what has been and is the
     Christian answer'. To deny this insight into the
     history of their society was to 'indoctrinate by
     default'.

70   Carpenter, H., *Robert Runcie: the reluctant
     archbishop*, London: Hodder and Stoughton, 1996,
     p. 159.

71   Carpenter, *Robert Runcie*, 1996, p. 159. David
     Jenkins was chaplain at Queen's College, Oxford.

72   The National Society, *One Hundred and Fifty-ninth
     Annual Report 1970*, London: The National Society,
     1970, p. 10.

73   The National Society, *Annual Report 1970*, p. 10.

74   Todd, N., 'The Church of England School: in pursuit
     of a Christian tradition', *Aspects of Education*, 35,
     University of Hull.

75   Manchester Diocesan Board of Education, Syllabus
     for Religious Education, 1994.

76   Chater, *Religion in Education*, Vol. I, 1997,
     pp. 261-63.

77   *Education for All: the report of the committee of
      inquiry into the education of children from minority
      ethnic groups*, (Swann report), Cmnd 9453, London:
      HMSO, March 1985.

78   Trevelyan's remarks on the familiarity of 'people of
      all classes' with the Bible in 1815, which 'raised their
      imaginations above insipid vulgarity of mind' must
      grate upon the ears of these writers.

79   Hyde, K.E., *Religious Learning in Adolescence*,
      University of Birmingham Institute of Education,
      Educational Monograph No. 7, London: Oliver and
      Boyd, 1965. Goldman, R.J., *Religious Thinking from
      Childhood to Adolescence*, London: Routledge and
      Kegan Paul, 1964. Goldman, R.J., *Readiness for
      Religion*, London: Routledge and Kegan Paul, 1965.

80   Hirst, P.H., 'Christian education: a contradiction in
      terms?', *Learning for Living*, 11, 1972. Hirst, P.H.,
      'Religious beliefs and educational principles',in
      Learning for Living, 15, 1976. The National Society,
      The Fourth R, (Durham report), London: The
      National Society and SPCK, 1970. *Children and their
      Primary Schools*, (Plowden report), London: HMSO,
      1967.

81   Schools Council, *Religious Education in Secondary
      Schools*, London: Evans Brothers and Methuen
      Educational, 1971. 'Confessional' is a term that is
      often found in discussions of post-1970 religious
      education in schools. But its meaning varies from, at
      one extreme, the indoctrination of 'Church of
      England' or 'Jewish' beliefs, and so forth,to the other
      extreme of any hint that religion is an especially good
      thing at all.

82   Loukes, H., *Teenage Religion*, London: SCM, 1961.
      Loukes, H., *New Ground in Christian Education*,
      London: SCM, 1965. Grimmitt, M., *What Can I Do in
      RE?* Great Wakering: McCrimmon, 1973. Grimmitt,
      M., *Religious Education and Human Development*,
      Great Wakering: McCrimmon, 1987. Holm, L.J.,
      Teaching Religion in School: a practical approach,
      London: OUP, 1975.

83   Longley, C., 'We need more belief, not more
      policemen', *Daily Telegraph*, 27 December 2000.

84   The Shap working party, *The Shap Handbook on World Religions in Education*, London: CRE, 1977.

85   Smart, N., *Secular Education and the Logic of Religion*, London: Faber, 1968. Smart, N. and Horder, D. (eds.), *New Movements in Religious Education*, London: Temple Smith, 1975. Smart, N., *The World's Religions*, Cambridge: CUP, 1989.

86   Chater, *Religion in Education*, Vol. I, 1997, p. 258.

87   Tingle, R., *Freedom Today*, 1988.

88   Schools Council, *Religious Education in Secondary Schools*, Working Paper 36, 1971.

89   Chater, *Religion in Education*, Vol. I, 1997, pp. 274-75.

90   'Preface', Agreed Syllabus for Religious Education in West Sussex Schools, 1983. Among other predominantly 'Christian' syllabuses are those of Northamptonshire (1980), Lincolnshire (1980) and Cambridgeshire (1982). Cambridgeshire's syllabus says that Christianity is the religion 'which will be studied in the greatest detail'.

91   *Brent Religious Education Today and Tomorrow*, 1985.

92   Norman, E.R., *Christianity and the World Order*, Oxford: Oxford University Press, 1979, pp. 18-19 and pp. 38-39. Norman's Reith lectures were immediately attacked in Elliott, C. and others, *Christian Faith and Political Hopes: a reply to E.R. Norman*, London: Epworth Press, 1979. The essayists included the sociologist Professor Robert Moore and Professor David Jenkins, later Bishop of Durham.

93   Whelan, R., (ed.), *Teaching Right and Wrong: have the churches failed?*, London: IEA Health and Welfare Unit, 1994.

94   Davies, J., 'Resacralising education', in Whelan, *Teaching Right and Wrong*, 1994, p. 11.

95   Norman, E.R., *Out of the Depths*, London: Continuum, 2001, Introduction.

96   Bruce, R. and Wallbank, J., *Beginning Religion*, London: Arnold, 1982.

97   Boyd, A., *Baroness Cox: a voice for the voiceless*, Oxford: Lion, 1998, pp. 423-24.

98   Boyd, *Baroness Cox*, 1998, p. 424.

99   Boyd, *Baroness Cox*, 1998, p. 425-26.

100   Wordsworth, *Works of William Wordsworth*, 1994, p. 433.

101   Longley, C., 'Dangers for a society that has lost its memory', *The Times*, 1 May 1988.

102   *The Times*, 3 May 1988.

103   *Hansard*, 130, 405.

104   *Hansard*, 130, 408.

105   *Hansard*, 130, 420-21, 425, 426.

106   *Hansard*, 130, 413.

107   *Church Times*, 13 May 1988. The Bishop of London, the report said, aimed to consult with local authorities, other faiths and the teaching profession to find an acceptable formula which would include the word Christian ready for the report stage on 20 June 1988.

108   Section 1.2 (a) and (b).

109   Educational Reform Act 1988, section 8 (3). Agreed syllabuses had to 'take into account' also 'the teaching and practices of other principal religions represented in Great Britain'. See also, *Hansard*, 21 June 1988, col. 639. An influential pamphlet had been produced by a head master and a teacher at Newcastle upon Tyne schools, Burn, J. and Hart, C., *The Crisis in Religious Education*, London: Educational Research Trust, 1988.

110   To remove all doubt that the meaning of the word 'denominations' had been changed, the DES Circular 3/89 makes it clear that 'other religious denominations' are likely to include non-Christian groups.

111   Section 9.

112   Though each SACRE was given the power to exempt schools or groups of pupils from Christian collective worship, it was not given the power to exempt them from classroom lessons. This seems to have been

simply an oversight in the drafting of the Act in its
final form.

113 House of Lords Official Report (Hansard), 7 July
1988, col. 442. The redundancy of the Cowper-Temple
clause had been pointed out by Lord Renton, and was
accepted by the government. The demise of Cowper-
Temple does not seem to have been connected with
the efforts of either the National Society, the Bishop
of London, or Baroness Cox. Section 26 of the 1988
Act states: 'No such syllabus shall provide for
religious education to be given to pupils at such a
school by means of any catechism or formulary which
is distinctive of any particular religious
denomination; but this provision is not to be taken as
prohibiting provision in such a syllabus for the study
of such catechisms or formularies'.

114 Department of Education and Science (DES),
Circular 1/89, London: DES, 20 January 1989, p. 33.

115 Archbishop's Council Church Schools Review Group,
Consultation Report December 2000, (Dearing report),
London: The Archbishop's Council, 2000, pp. 13-15.
Even this strong statement is not quite free of the
relativism it deplores. It says that the school will be
'quietly respectful' of the beliefs of others. Respect,
quiet or otherwise, of *all* beliefs, cannot be desirable
in any society or organisation within it. The point is
to be open to persuasion from all quarters. The first
step in being persuaded is coming to the conclusion
that what the other person is doing or saying is
worthy of respect. Of course, to be respectful of the
person as a human being, irrespective of one's respect
for his or her beliefs and actions is another matter
altogether.

116 Church Schools Review Group, *Consultation Report*,
2000, p. 9.

117 Church Schools Review Group, *Consultation Report*,
2000, p. 13.

118 Department for Education and Employment (DfEE),
Schools: Building on Success (green paper), London:
DfEE, 12 February 2001.

NOTES 143

119 Archbishop's Council Church Schools Review Group, *The Way Ahead: Church of England schools in the new millennium*, (Dearing report), London: Church House Publishing, 2001.

120 Church Schools Review Group, *The Way Ahead*, 2001, pp. 30-31.

121 Church Schools Review Group, *The Way Ahead*, 2001, pp. 16-17.

122 Church Schools Review Group, *The Way Ahead*, 2001, pp. 20-21.

123 Church Schools Review Group, *The Way Ahead*, 2001, pp. 14-15.

124 *Religious Education and School Worship in the 1988 Education Act*, London: The National Society, 1988, p. 6.

125 *Guardian*, 22 June 1988.

126 *Independent*, 31 January 1994.

127 'Teaching religious education', *Education*, 18 November 1988, p. i.

128 *Education*, 1988. p. iv.

129 *Education*, 1988, p. ii.

130 This journal originated as *Religion In Education* in 1936 as the organ of the Institute of Christian Education, the forerunner of the Christian Education Movement. It was renamed the *British Journal of Religious Education (BJRE)* in 1978.

131 Speech given by the Chief Executive of the City of Birmingham, Sir Michael Lyons, reported in the *Daily Telegraph*, 8 December 2000. The figure was exceeded by Leicester where 45 per cent of the schoolchildren were non-white.

132 *BJRE*, 11, 1, Autumn 1988. Emphasis added. Hull, J.M., *Mishmash: religious education in multicultural Britain—a study in metaphor*, Birmingham: University of Birmingham School of Education, 1991.

133 Hull, J.M., *The Act Unpacked: the meaning of the 1988 Education Reform Act for religious education*, University of Birmingham and CEM, 1989, p. 14.

134 As distinct from acts of worship not 'in the normal run'—what the legislation calls 'determinations'. 'Determinations' are acts of worship exclusive to a particular faith.

135 *BJRE*, 11, 3, 1989.

136 Section 10 (1) (b).

137 Religious Education Council of England and Wales, *Time for Religious Education and Teachers to Match: a digest of underprovision*, Lancaster: St. Martin's College, 1993.

138 *Independent*, 3 June 1994.

139 Department of Education and Science letter to Chief Education Officers, 18 March 1991. Emphasis added.

140 National Curriculum Council (NCC), *Analysis of Agreed Syllabuses*, London: DFE, 1993. The syllabuses lacked content on the other 'principal faiths' too.

141 *The Times*, 10 April 1993.

142 *Sunday Telegraph*, 2 January 1994.

143 *Guardian*, 25 January 1994.The final version of the national model syllabuses were published on 5 July 1994.

144 Department for Education (DFE), *Religious Education and Collective Worship*, London: DFE, 1994, Circular 1-94. *The Times*, 10 April 1993. *Sunday Telegraph*, 2 January 1994. *Guardian*, 25 January 1994.The final version of the national model syllabuses were published on 5 July 1994. DFE, *Religious Education and Collective Worship*, 1994.

145 QCA website (www.qca.org.uk), 8 February 2001.

146 See, for example, Weber, M., 'Politics as a vocation' (1918), in Gerth, H. and Mills, C.W., *From Max Weber: essays in sociology*, New York: Oxford University Press, 1946.

147 Temple, *Citizen and Churchman*, 1941, p. 27.

3: Church of England School Provision

1 Trevelyan, G.M., *English Social History: a survey of six centuries from Chaucer to Queen Victoria* (1942), London: Penguin, 1986, pp. 279-80.

2 Mill, J., *Edinburgh Review*, October 1813. Emphasis added. Mill, J., *Westminster Review*, October 1826. Cited in West, E.G., *Education and the State: a study in political economy* (1965), 2nd edn., London: IEA, 1970, p. 136.

3 'Report on the state of education in the borough of Kingston upon Hull', *Journal of the Statistical Society of London*, July 1841.

4 Kay, J.P., 'The training of pauper children', *Report of the Poor Law Commissioners*, 1841. Kay's figures refer to 9 to 16 year olds in the workhouses of Norfolk and Suffolk in 1838. Kay became the first secretary to the Education Committee of the Privy Council in 1839.

5 West, E.G., *Education and the State: a study in political economy* (1965), 2nd edn, London: IEA, 1970, pp. 126-30.

6 West, *Education and the State*, 1970, p. 131.

7 Webb, R.K., 'Working class readers in early Victorian England', *The English Historical Review*, 1950, p. 337. See also, Webb, R.K., 'The Victorian reading public', *From Dickens to Hardy*, Harmondsworth: Pelican, 1963.

8 Altick, R.D., *The English Common Reader*, Chicago: University of Chicago Press, 1957, p. 171. Cited in West, *Education and the State*, 1970, pp. 134-35. Emphasis added.

9 Williams, R., *The Long Revolution*, London: Chatto and Windus, 1961, p. 166.

10 *Report of the Parliamentary Committee on the Education of the Lower Orders in the Metropolis and Beyond*, 1818. The work of the committee had been promoted by Henry Brougham.

11 *Report of the Parliamentary Committee on the State of Education*, 1834.

12   House of Lords, 21 May 1835.

13   West, *Education and the State*, 1970, pp. 137-38.
      Fuller details on the growth of the school population
      1800-1840 are provided in West, E.G., 'Resource
      allocation and growth in the early nineteenth
      century', *Economic History Review*, April 1970.

14   *Census 1851*, pp. cxxxiv-v. Cited in West, *Education
      and the State*, 1970, p. 140.

15   *Report of the Commissioners Appointed to Enquire
      into the State of Popular Education in England*,
      (Newcastle Commission), Vol. 1, London: HMSO,
      1861, p. 86.

16   Trevelyan. G.M., *British History in the Nineteenth
      Century and After* (1922), Harmondsworth: Penguin,
      1965, p. 354. Emphasis added.

17   West, *Education and the State*, 1970, pp. 144-46.

18   *Report of the Education Department of the Privy
      Council*, annually until 1899. Between 1870 and
      1895 the School Boards produced school accom-
      modation for 2.2 million pupils. Not all were new
      schools. The Boards 'acquired a considerable number
      of schools, either by arrangement with private
      owners ... or, where premises were held in trust for
      educational purposes, by transfer ... under the Act of
      1870'. As well as the 792 Church of England schools,
      223 British schools and 15 Wesleyan schools were
      transferred 1870-1886. *Report of the Committee of
      Council on Education*, 1886, pp. xi-xii. Cited in West,
      Education and the State, 1970, p. 149.

19   Balfour, A.J., in a speech introducing the 1902
      Education Bill, 24 March 1902.

20   The school figures are those given by Balfour in the
      speech.

21   Archbishop's Council Church Schools Review Group,
      *The Way Ahead: Church of England schools in the
      new millennium*, (Dearing report), London: Church
      House Publishing, 2001, p. 7. See also Murphy, J.,
      Church, State and Schools in Britain 1800-1900,
      London: Routledge and Kegan Paul, 1971, p. 125.
      Department for Education and Science (DES), *School
      Statistics*, London: DES, Table A 12/92.

NOTES

4: The Civilisation Motive

1   Halsey, A.H., Floud, J. and Anderson, C.A.,
    *Education, Economy and Society: a reader in the
    sociology of education*, New York: Free Press, 1961,
    pp. 391-523.

2   Glass, D.V., 'Education and social change in modern
    England', in Halsey, Floud, and Anderson,
    Education, Economy and Society, 1961, p. 395. Until
    1944 most working-class children received an
    'elementary' and 'senior elementary' school education
    up to the age of 14. 'Secondary' education was
    obtained by only a few of them in the 'special places'
    of the grammar schools.

3   Adamson, J.W., *English Education 1789-1902*,
    Cambridge: CUP, 1902, p. 210. Emphasis added.

4   National Education Union, *A Verbatim Report of the
    Debate in Parliament during the Progress of the
    Education Bill, 1870*, Manchester: National
    Education Union, no date, pp. 5 and 18.

5   Engels says 'until 15 years ago'. He had in mind the
    (from the point of view of the revolution) hopeful
    incidents of unrest of the 1880s, few and orderly by
    the standards of the 1980s and later. Their children
    had failed the revolutionaries of the 1840s, Engels
    said, but their grandchildren would not.

6   Engels, F., 'Introduction to socialism: utopian and
    scientific' (1892), in *K. Marx, and F. Engels on
    Religion*, Moscow: Foreign Languages Publishing
    House, 1957, p. 306. Emphasis added. Engels' com-
    ments on the 'crime-ridden' England of 1844 is
    interesting as a contrast with England in 2001. In his
    The Condition of the Working Class he depicts in the
    darkest shades all that was wrong with England in
    1844.'With the extension of the proletariat', Engels
    writes, 'crime has increased in England, and the British
    nation has become the most criminal in the world.' He
    points out that most offences were *not* of violence, but
    against property, *'as in all civilized countries'*. 'I look at a
    random heap of English journals lying before me', he
    writes. 'There is the *Manchester Guardian* for October
    30, 1844, which reports for three days that in Salford a
    couple of boys had been caught stealing, and a

bankrupt tradesman tried to cheat his creditors.' In
Ashton in the course of three days there were two
thefts, one burglary, and one suicide. In Bury there was
one theft. In Bolton there were two thefts and one
revenue fraud. In Leigh in the course of three days
there was one theft. In Oldham, the scene of savage
rioting in May 2001 (see the national newspapers of 28
May 2001) what shocked Engels in 1844 was that in the
course of three days there had been one theft, one fight
between Irish women, one non-union hatter assaulted
by union men, one mother beaten by her son, one attack
upon the police, and one robbery of a church. In
Stockport there was discontent of working men with
wages, one theft, one fraud, one fight, and one wife
beaten by her husband. In Warrington there was one
theft, and one fight. In Wigan there was one fight, and
one robbery of a church. In London, he writes, the
position is much worse so far as crime is concerned. In a
single day, according to reports Engels gleaned from *The
Times*, there was in the whole of London no fewer than
one theft, one attack upon the police, a sentence upon a
father requiring him to support his illegitimate son, the
abandonment of a child by his parents, and the
poisoning of a man by his wife. 'Similar reports', he
says, 'are to be found in all the English papers',
sufficient evidence, if evidence were needed, that 'in this
country, social war is under full headway'. Engels, F.,
The Condition of the Working Class in England in 1844
(1845), London: Allen and Unwin, 1892, pp. 131-32.

7   Trotsky, L., *Where is Britain Going?* (1925), London:
New Park, 1978. The 'pigsty of Parliamentary
democracy' is Lenin's phrase. Lenin, V.I., 'The state
and revolution' (1917), in *Collected Works II*, Moscow:
Foreign Languages Publishing House, 1947, p. 171.

8   Evans, J.E., *Twelve Talks on Christian Citizenship
for Leaders of Youth*, London: Christian Social
Council, no date, p. 64. The pamphlet refers to the
'recent' ascent of the Matterhorn by the one-legged
climber, George Winthrop Young.

9   Norwood, C., *The English Tradition of Education*,
London: John Murray, 1929, pp. 171-72.

NOTES 149

10 Lowndes, G.A.N., *The Silent Social Revolution: an account of the expansion of public education in England and Wales 1895-1935*, London: OUP, 1937, p. 239. Emphasis added.

11 Lowndes, *The Silent Social Revolution*, 1937, p. 239. Emphasis added.

12 *Libération*, 23 February 2001. See also Cohn-Bendit, D, *Le Grand Bazar,* 1975.

13 Womack, S., 'Teachers get self-defence lessons in £22m safety plan', *Daily Telegraph*, 29 December 2000.

5: The Culture Wars 1950 - 2001

1 Wordsworth, W., 'Childhood and school-time', *The Prelude* (1799), in *The Works of William Wordsworth*, Ware: Wordsworth editions, 1994, p. 432.

2 To mark the end of his first year in office, an Archbishop of Canterbury assured the British people that the Church of England was just as *guilty* as 'any other section of the community' in thinking that sexual sins were more significant than any other sin. (*Independent*, 20 March 1992.) Did he indeed feel that *condemnation* of sexual permissiveness was the evil that the Church of England was called upon at that juncture to correct? Were not 'sections of community' daily and powerfully propagating the same message, that it was condemnation of sexual sins that was wrong; what was right was any sex in any context, and sex was never a sin at all?

3 'Hell' is in italics here because it appears from the title that Blake, a Christian, did not approve of them. The 'Proverbs of Hell' are now frequently quoted as if he did approve of them.

4 Sowell, T., *A Conflict of Visions*, New York: Morrow Quill, 1987.

5 I Corinthians 12, 4-6.

6 Durkheim, E., *The Elementary Forms of the Religious Life* (1912), London: Allen and Unwin, 1915. On Durkheim's educational views, see his *Education and Sociology* (1922), Glencoe, Ill: Free Press, 1956.

7   Otto, R., *The Idea of the Holy*, Oxford: OUP, 1923, p. 279.

8   Marx, K. and Engels, F., *The Communist Manifesto*, in Marx, K. and Engels, F., *Selected Works I*, Moscow: Foreign Languages Publishing House, 1958, p. 37.

9   Engels, F., 'Introduction to socialism: utopian and scientific' (1892), in Marx, K. and Engels, F., *On Religion*, Moscow: Foreign Languages Publishing House, 1957, p. 306.

10   Frazer, J.G., *The Golden Bough: a study in comparative religion* (1890), London: Macmillan, 1911-15.

11   Weber, M., *Economy and Society: an outline of interpretive sociology* (1922), Berkeley: University of California Press, 1978, Vol. I, p. 422.

12   A classic study of magic is Malinowski, B., *Coral Gardens and their Magic*, London: Allen and Unwin, 1935.

13   Nietzsche, F., *The Birth of Tragedy from the Spirit of Music* (1872), New York: 1924. Ruth Benedict used this dichotomy to structure her celebrated study of the Dobu, the Kwakiutl and the Zuñi. Benedict, R., *Patterns of Culture* (1934), New York, Mentor, 1959.

14   Nietzsche, *Birth of Tragedy*, 1924, p. 40. Nietzsche, F., *Thus Spake Zarathustra* (1883-85), London: Dent, 1957.

15   Nietzsche, *Birth of Tragedy*, 1924, p. 68.

16   Trevelyan, G.M., *English Social History: a survey of six centuries from Chaucer to Queen Victoria* (1942), Harmondsworth: Penguin, 1986, p. 276. Emphasis added. Trevelyan was a figure revered by the Labour party of R.H. Tawney—the dominant working-class movement of the time. His brother, Sir Charles Trevelyan, was the first Labour Minister of Education. G.M. Trevelyan was prominent in three of the Labour party's most sacred causes (in the sense that they were good beyond question): the widest opportunities and highest standards of education and 'culture' (in the sense of refinement) for working -class children; the National Trust; and the Youth Hostels Association, of which he was President from

1930 to 1950. He died in 1962, the same year as R.H. Tawney died, so they saw (if they did see them) only the first shoots of an English 'culture' (in the sense of private and public beliefs and conduct) which contains so much of what they publicly detested and had thought England was safely past.

17   Fletcher, A., Letter to the Marquis of Monroe and others, Andrew Fletcher of Saltoun.

18   Pook, S., 'Sex shop fined because its videos are "too tame"', *Daily Telegraph*, 19 January 2001.

19   *Underage Drinking: findings from the 1998-99 Youth Lifestyles Survey*, Home Office Research, Development and Statistics Directorate Research Findings No. 125, London: Home Office, 2000.

20   World Health Organisation (WHO), *Drinking Among Young Europeans*, Geneva: WHO, February 2001. In Europe, the figures were higher only in Greece and Italy. The WHO was principally concerned with the physical health aspects of childhood alcohol consumption, claiming in this report that in Europe 15,000 males aged 15-29 died annually as the result of excessive drinking, one-quarter of the age-group deaths.

21   Godwin, W., *Enquiry Concerning Political Justice* (1798), London: Penguin, 1985. It is antiquated in the purely chronological sense that it stems from the end of the eighteenth century. But it is even more antiquated in the social sense. By the standards of the end of the twentieth century and the beginning of the twenty-first, it is extremely moralistic and 'judgemental'.

22   Godwin, *Enquiry Concerning Political Justice*, 1985. Quoted by Sowell, *Conflict of Visions*, 1987, pp. 23-25.

23   Crosland, A., *The Future of Socialism*, London: Jonathan Cape, 1956.

24   J. Adington Symonds, 1840-93. This was a familiar hymn in many working-class chapels, and eventually found its way into *Songs of Praise*. See also, in the 1931 edition of *Songs of Praise*, such altruistic socialist hymns as Walt Whitman's 'Pioneers'—often

seen on trade union banners—'We take up the task
eternal, and the burden, and the lesson ... ' (304);
G.K. Chesterton's 'The walls of gold entomb us ... '
(308); J. Russell Lowell's 'Once to every man and
nation/Comes the moment to decide,/In the strife of
truth with falsehood,/For the good or evil side ... '
(309); the Christian socialist Charles Kingsley's 'The
nations sleep starving on heaps of gold ... ' (310);
Shelley's, 'Another Athens shall arise ... ' (311)—
Shelley was Godwin's son-in-law; Massey's 'Through
all the long dark night of years/The people's cry
ascendeth ... ', with its cry to 'build up heroic lives'
(313); Ebenezer Elliot's 'When wilt thou save the
people?/ ... Not throne and crowns, but men!?'—Elliot
was the poet of Chartism; or the Fabian Carpenter's
'England, arise! the long, long night is over ... ' (316).

25   'To feel much for others and little for ourselves ... to
restrain our selfish, and to indulge our benevolent,
affections, constitutes the perfection of human
nature; and can alone produce among mankind that
harmony of sentiments and passions in which
consists their whole grace and propriety.' Smith, A.,
The Theory of Moral Sentiments (1759), Indianapolis:
Liberty, 1976, pp. 71-72.

26   Smith, *Theory of Moral Sentiments*, 1976, p. 284.

27   Smith, *Theory of Moral Sentiments*, 1976, pp. 233-34.

28   He was not denounced for his code of morality.
Pelegius preached Christian asceticism. On the
choices that people did make he was, like Godwin,
highly moralistic and judgemental.

29   Tocqueville, A. de, *Democracy in America* (Part II
1840), New York: Mentor, 1956.

30   Durkheim, E., *The Division of Labour in Society*
(1893), London: Macmillan, 1933.

31   For example, Arendt, H., *The Origins of Totalitarianism* (1951), New York: Meridian, 1958.

32   Arendt, *The Origins of Totalitarianism*, 1958, p. 485.

33   In a speech to the British-German Society,
25 January 2001.

34   Cooley, C.H., *Social Organisation: a study of the larger mind*, New York: Scribner, 1909. Emphasis added.

35   Lipset, S.M., *Political Man*, London: Heinemann, 1960. Bendix, R. and Lipset, S.M., 'Political sociology', *Current Sociology*, 6, 2, 1957.

36   Aron, R., *Main Currents of Sociological Thought: Comte, vol. I Montesquieu, Marx, Tocqueville* (1965), Harmondsworth: Penguin, 1968.

37   Mills, C. W., 'Mass society and liberal education' (1952), in Mills, C. W., *Power, Politics and People: the collected essays of C. Wright Mills*, New York: Oxford University Press, 1963, p. 353 and p. 357. Emphasis added.

38   Lipset, S.M., Trow, M. and Coleman, J., *Union Democracy: the inside politics of the International Typographical Union*, Glencoe, Ill: Free Press, 1956, p. 15. Emphasis added.

39   Aron, *Main Currents of Sociological Thought*, Vol. I, 1968, p. 202.

40   Mills, *Power, Politics and People*, 1963, p. 370.

41   Fukuyama, F., *The Great Disruption: human nature and the reconstitution of social order*, New York: Free Press, pp. 10-11. Emphasis added. His other two books were *The End of History and the Last Man*, New York: Free Press, 1992; and *Trust: the social virtues and the creation of prosperity*, New York: Free Press, 1995.

42   Tocqueville, *Democracy in America*, 1956. p. 296. Emphasis added.

43   Bestor, A.E., *Educational Wastelands: the retreat from learning in our public schools*, Urbana: University of Illinois Press, 1953, p. 7.

44   St Augustine, *Concerning the City of God against the Pagans* (413-27), London: Penguin, 1984, pp. 833-34.

45   Second Vatican Council, *Declaration on Christian Education—Gravissimum Educationis*, October 1965.

46   Earlier he had said, in an interview on Irish Radio in
      January 1998, that it was a 'sham' for Roman
      Catholics to receive Holy Communion in a reformed
      church.

47   *Irish Independent*, 19 February 2001. The editorial
      subtly said that Archbishop Connell, 'should not
      attempt to make other persuasions cooperate in
      imposing his rules'.

48   *British Journal of Religious Education (BJRE)*. 11, 1,
      Autumn 1988. Emphasis added.

49   Tocqueville, *Democracy in America* , 1956, p. 314.

6: The Sociology of Post-1970 Religious Education

1   Weber, M., *Economy and Society: an outline of
      interpretive sociology* (1922), Berkeley: University of
      California Press, 1978; for his sociology of religion in
      Economy and Society, see Vol. I, pp. 399-634. Weber,
      M., *The Protestant Ethic and the Spirit of Capitalism*
      (1904), London: Allen and Unwin, 1930. Weber M.,
      The Hindu Social System, (1920-21), Minneapolis:
      University of Minnesota Sociology Club, 1950.
      Weber, M., *The Religion of China: Confucianism and
      Taoism* (1920-21), Glencoe, Ill: The Free Press, 1951.
      Weber, M., *Ancient Judaism* (1920-21), Glencoe, Ill:
      The Free Press, 1952. Weber, M., *The Religion of
      India* (1920-21), Glencoe, Ill: The Free Press, 1958.

2   Weber, *The Protestant Ethic*, 1930.

3   Weber, M., 'Politics as a vocation' (1918), in Gerth, H.
      and Mills, C.W., *From Max Weber: essays in
      sociology*, New York: Oxford University Press, 1946.

4   Weber, 'Science as a vocation' (1919), in Gerth and
      Mills, *From Max Weber*, 1946.

5   Troeltsch, E., *The Social Teaching of the Christian
      Churches* (1931), Chicago: University of Chicago
      Press, 1981.

6   Mannheim, K., *Ideology and Utopia: an introduction
      to the sociology of knowledge*, (1929-31), London:
      Kegan Paul, Trench, Trubner, 1936. He sought to
      understand both the general view of the world and
      eternity of each (the sociologist's process of
      sinngemässe Zurechnung), and the way in which this

NOTES 155

general view was expressed in particular areas of the conservative's and liberal's life (the sociologist's process of *Faktizitätszurechnung*), pp. 276-77.

7   The control of unlawful conduct by the state by the exercise of its monopoly of legitimate force is a large question that does not arise here, where the subject is opinion and not action. What expressions of opinion in certain contexts can be correctly controlled by the state, if any, and if anywhere, within the general rule that the state does not control opinion, is another question that lies outside the scope of this chapter.

8   Examples of such Weberian sociology in my own work are the study of the way the miners of a coal-mining town looked at the world in the 1950s, Dennis, N., Slaughter, C. and Henriques, F., *Coal is Our Life*, London: Eyre and Spottiswoode, 1956. Two books on Sunderland deal with the contrasting world-views of professional town planners and residents of a slum clearance district, Dennis, N., *People and Planning*, London: Faber and Faber, 1970, and Dennis, N., *Public Participation and Planners' Blight*, London: Faber and Faber, 1972. The world-view of the 'ethical socialist'—Labour up to the early 1960s—is analysed in Dennis, N. and Halsey, A.H., *English Ethical Socialism*, Oxford: Clarendon, 1988.

9   Weber, M., *The Theory of Social and Economic Organisation*, New York: The Free Press, 1947, pp. 87-120.

10   Weber, 'Politics as a vocation' (1918), Gerth and Mills, *From Max Weber*, 1946.

11   Weber, M., *Parlament und Regierung im neugeordneten Deutschland*, Munich: Duncker and Humboldt, 1918. (This originated as an article praising England's political culture and institutions as compared with Germany's: 'Parliament and government in a reformed Germany', published in a Munich newspaper in 1916.)

12   Hick, J. and Knitter, P.F. (eds.), *The Myth of Christian Uniqueness: toward a pluralistic theology of religions*, London: SCM, 1988.

13   Sacks, J.,' The Reith Lectures 1990: lecture four',
      Listener, 6 December 1990, p. 18. Emphasis added.

14   Popper, K.R., *The Open Society and its Enemies*, 5th
      edn., London: Routledge, 1966.

15   Kay, W.K. and Francis, L.J. (eds.), *Religion in
      Education*, Vol. I, Leominster, Herefordshire:
      Gracewing, 1997, *passim*.

16   One sometimes yearns to put that question in a *viva
      voce* to some of the people who pepper their works on
      the beauties of 'phenomenological' religious
      education in schools with his name.

17   Husserl, E., 'Phenomenology', *Encyclopædia
      Britannica*, 14th edn., 1929. Husserl, M., *Ideen zu
      einer reinen Phänomenolgie und phänomenolgischen
      Philosophie*, Halle a d S: Niemeyer, 1913. Husserl,
      E., *Ideas: general introduction to pure phenomenology*
      (1913), London: 1931. Husserl, E., *The Idea of
      Phenomenology*, The Hague: Nijhoff, 1964. Husserl,
      E., *Phenomenology and the Crisis of Philosophy*, New
      York: Harper, Row, 1965.

18   Husserl, *Ideas*, 1931, p. 11.

19   Husserl, *Ideas*, 1931, p. 29.

20   Husserl, *Ideas*, 1931, pp. 17-18. The punctuation in
      Ideas is as reproduced here. Emphasis added.

21   Bettis, J. (ed.), *Phenomenology of Religion*, London:
      SCM, 1969. Chater, M., 'Philosophy of religious
      education', in Kay, W.K and Francis, L.J. (eds.),
      Religion in Education, Vol. I, Leominster,
      Herefordshire: Gracewing, 1997, pp. 272-73. On St.
      Herbert, see Wordsworth, W., 'Inscriptions XV'.

22   Chater, *Religion in Education*, Vol. I, 1997, p. 274.

23   Chater, *Religion in Education*, Vol. I, 1997, p. 273.

24   Leeuw, G. van der, *Religion in Essence and
      Manifestation a study in phenomenology*, London:
      Allen and Unwin, 1938. p. 646.

25   Chater, *Religion in Education*, Vol. I, 1997, p. 301.
      Chater refers here to Watson, B., *The Effective
      Teaching of Religious Education*, London: Longman,
      1993, and Read, G., Rudge, J. and Howarth, R.B.,

How Do I Teach RE?, London: Mary Glasgow
Publications, 1986.

26   Chater, *Religion in Education*, Vol. I, 1997,
      pp. 301-02 and p. 305. Emphasis added. The Westhill
      Project, in general a moderate version of the new 'RE'
      produced a teacher's handbook on the world religions
      approach, with pupils' textbooks, and photopacks to
      cover all four Key Stages from age five to 16. The one
      main aim, the handbook of the Westhill Project says,
      is to help children mature in relation to 'their own
      pattern of belief and behaviour' through exploring
      other people's religious beliefs and practices (and
      related human experiences—social phenomena that
      are like religions). Westhill Project, *How Do I Teach
      RE?*, (no bibliographical details supplied).

27   Chater, *Religion in Education*, Vol. I, 1997, p. 304.

28   *How Do I Teach RE?*, p. 25.

29   Chater, *Religion in Education*, Vol. I, 1997,
      pp. 304-05.

30   *How Do I Teach RE?*, pp. 30-31. Cited in Chater,
      Religion in Education, Vol. I, 1997, p. 305.

31   *Education of Children from Minority Ethnic Groups*,
      1985. (Place of publication and publisher not
      supplied.)

32   Chater, *Religion in Education*, Vol. I, 1997, p. 304.
      Emphasis added.

33   James, W., *The Varieties of Religious Experience*,
      Glasgow: Collins, 1902.

34   Robinson, E., *The Original Vision: a study of the
      religious experience of childhood*, Oxford: Religious
      Experience Research Unit, 1977. Hay, D., *Exploring
      Inner Space*, Harmondsworth: Penguin, 1982.

35   Hammond, J., Hay, D., Moxon, J., Netto, B., Raban,
      K., Straugheir, G. and Williams, C., *New Methods in
      RE Teaching: an experiential approach*, Harlow:
      Oliver and Boyd, 1990.

36   Chater, *Religion in Education*, Vol. I, 1997, pp.
      282-83 and pp. 307-10. Emphasis added. He asks, 'Is
      it a stalking horse for an inappropriate return to
      confessionalism?', that is, to the teaching of some

form of Christianity (or Islam, or Judaism, as the case may be).

37   School Curriculum and Assessment Authority (SCAA), *Spiritual and Moral Development*, London: SCAA, 1995.

38   Lealman, B. (ed.), *What is RE?: a guide for parents, governors and teachers*, London: British Council of Churches Religious Education Consultants Group and the Christian Education Movement (CEM), 1984. *Exploring a Theme: water*. London: CEM, no date shown. *Exploring a Theme: fire*, London: CEM, no date shown. *Exploring a Theme: places of worship*, London: CEM, no date shown. The role of the Christian teacher in relation to the world-religions theme is continued in Johnson, C., *Christian Teachers and World Faiths*, London: CEM, 1996.

39   Rogers, C.R., *A Therapist's View of Personal Goals*, Wallingford, Pa: Pendle Hill, 1977. Rogers, C.R., *A Way of Being*, Boston, Mass: Houghton Mifflin, 1980. Rogers, C.R., *The Carl Rogers Reader*, Kirschenbaum, H. and Henderson, V.L. (eds.), London: Constable, 1990. Penguin published a book in the mid-1970s in which Maslow related his ideas to religion. Maslow, A.H., *Religion, Values and Peak Experiences*, Harmondsworth: Penguin, 1976.

40   Rogers, C.R., *The Effective Teacher: a person-centred development guide*, Sheffield: PAVIC, 1982. Rogers, C.R., *Freedom to Learn for the Eighties*, London: Merrill, 1983.

41   MORI, *Easter Poll Research Study 21 March 1991*, 1991.

42   'Just Another Sunday', Radio 5live, 10 April 1994.

43   *The Times Educational Supplement*, December 1985.

44   *Hansard*, 23 March 1988, col. 403.

45   *The Times Educational Supplement*, 4 March 1988.

46   Chater, *Religion in Education*, Vol. I, 1997, p. 272. Emphasis in original.

47   Acton, J., *The History of Freedom and Other Essays*, London: Macmillan, 1907, p. 52.

48 Holloway, D., *Church and State in the New Millennium: issues of belief and morality for the 21st century*, London: HarperCollins, 2000, p. 122. Emphasis added.

Index